THE MEDIEVAL CASTLES OF WALES

THE MEDIEVAL CASTLES OF WALES

JOHN R. KENYON

UNIVERSITY OF WALES PRESS
CARDIFF
2010

www.uwp.co.uk

British Library Cataloguing-in-Publication Data
A catalogue record for this book is available from the British Library.

ISBN 978-0-7083-2180-5
e-ISBN 978-0-7083-2363-2

Printed by CPI Antony Rowe, Chippenham, Wiltshire

Richard – I hope that you approve, old friend!

Contents

Acknowledgements

My initial thanks must go to Sarah Lewis and Ennis Akpinar of the University of Wales Press for inviting me to contribute a book on castles. Sian Rees and Rick Turner kindly examined my proposed list of castles for inclusion here and made various suggestions to which I heeded. Rick also provided much assistance concerning developments and phasing at Caerphilly.

University of Wales Press and I acknowledge the generous support of Cadw, the historic environment service of the Welsh Assembly Government, for providing photographs and plans for this book. Diane Williams and Chris Kenyon assisted with the majority of the illustrations, and I am extremely grateful to them for their assistance, and also my thanks to Pete Lawrence, who produced the figures. Similarly, Penny Icke of the Royal Commission on the Ancient and Historical Monuments of Wales provided other illustrations, and I am indebted to her also. Neither organization bears any responsibility for the text.

I must also acknowledge the excellent resources of the Library of Amgueddfa Cymru-National Museum Wales, which augmented a not inconsiderable library at home!

My main debt is to Bill Zajac who somehow found the time, in an extremely busy year, to read through the preliminary draft of the whole book, and who made several suggestions, as well as corrections. This guide would have been the poorer without his input. Any errors that remain should, of course, be laid firmly at the door of the author.

Illustrations

Colour plates 3–12, 15, 16 and all the figures are © Cadw, Welsh Assembly Government (Crown Copyright). Colour plates 1, 2, 13 and 14 are © Royal Commission on the Ancient and Historical Monuments of Wales (Crown Copyright).

Colour Plates (between pages 22–23 and 86–87)

Figures

1

Introduction

Wales has long been considered the land of the castle, with the castles of Edward I in north Wales always capturing the imagination, coupled with a number of great strongholds in south Wales such as Chepstow and Pembroke. It has been calculated that over four hundred castles still survive in the country, varying from earthworks to great stone fortresses, but, to put that into perspective, the bordering Marcher counties of Herefordshire and Shropshire, whose medieval history is linked closely to events in Wales, together have almost two hundred surviving castles, whilst a further 240 are scattered across the English counties of Northumberland and Yorkshire. Yet it is the sheer magnificence of a large number of the castles in Wales that make this country a favourite for castle explorers. No less important is the splendour of the location of a number of them, from Harlech in the north-west, Castell y Bere in mid Wales, to Carreg Cennen in the south-west and Chepstow in the south-east.

This book is intended to be an authoritative short guide for the visitor to the history and architecture of the majority of the accessible medieval castles of Wales. Space does not allow a mention of all the castles that might be visited, and the choice is subjective, for which the author makes no apology! An example of an omission is the important stronghold of Cardigan, acquired by Ceredigion County Council in 2003, but a site that needs much conservation work before it can be fully opened to the public. The individual entries should be detailed enough for a visitor to understand a castle he or she is visiting, although few plans are included here, but where there is a guidebook the visitor will always find additional information, and many sites have interpretation panels displayed in key areas.

At one time or another, I have visited most of the castles described here, but this book could not have been written without the help of the superb guidebooks produced by Cadw, the surveys undertaken in the second half of the twentieth century by the Royal Commission on the

Ancient and Historical Monuments of Wales and a wealth of learned papers published in various archaeological and historical journals. In order to enable the reader to pursue the subject further, an outline of the key sources of information will be found in the Further Reading section.

The majority of the sites are of stone, varying from maintained ruins such as Caerphilly to roofed strongholds that have evolved into country houses, Chirk being a good example. Some of these masonry castles developed from what were originally earth-and-timber defences, but there are numerous others in Wales, not described here, that never went beyond the earth-and-timber stage, whether motte and bailey or ringwork. Some of the sites are now nothing more than fortified manors, but are included, although I have omitted the fortified enclosure associated with Ewenny Priory in the Vale of Glamorgan.

An outline of the development of the castle in the Middle Ages

This introduction summarizes the key developments in castle architecture in the Middle Ages. Some, but by no means all, of the key features to be found in a castle are also described in box features in the following pages.

The simplest definition of a castle, and one that by and large still holds true, is that it is the fortified residence of a lord. A castle could also be used as a centre of administration. Castles were introduced into England by the Normans at the time of the conquest in 1066, although a small number had been constructed in the 1050s, for example in Herefordshire, by the Norman favourites of the Saxon king of England, Edward the Confessor. The Normans' castles in England were erected in such cities as London and York, and several made use of existing fortifications such as Roman forts as can be seen at Portchester in Hampshire, or were built on the estates acquired as part of the conquest and settlement of England.

It was in the reigns of the first two Norman kings of England, William I (1066–87) and William II (1087–1100), that the first castles appeared in Wales as the Normans began to occupy various parts of south Wales and the border with England, the Welsh March. The Normans were also involved in a short-lived campaign in north Wales, which saw the construction of two of the finest accessible mottes, Aberlleiniog on Anglesey and Rhuddlan (Twthill) in Flintshire. These northern gains were soon lost to the resurgent Welsh, and even in their outposts in south-west Wales the Normans lost all their castles for a short period, apart from Pembroke. It was not until the death of Rhys ap Tewdwr, king of Deheubarth in south-west Wales, in 1093 that the Normans made major advances across south Wales. However, the Anglo-Norman subjugation of Wales was a long, drawn-out affair, one that lasted two centuries, culminating in the conquest of north Wales by King Edward I (1272–1307). However, one should not think of these centuries as a period of constant military campaigning, nor one of total domination by one side or the other. There were, however, long periods of ascendancy by Welsh rulers, such as the Lord Rhys (d.1193) in south-west Wales and the two Llywelyns of the house of Gwynedd in the north, Llywelyn ab Iorwerth, the Great (d.1240), and his grandson, Llywelyn ap Gruffudd (d.1282).

In a country divided into a number of kingdoms, often with one Welsh ruler pitted against another, and little in the way of national unity, it is not surprising that the Welsh response to the Normans was slow. Castles were attacked, some even taken and possibly occupied, but we do not have a record of the Welsh building castles themselves

Mottes, ringworks and baileys

The first castles in Britain, unless they made use of existing defences such as Roman forts, were mainly mottes, mounds somewhat akin to Christmas puddings, and fine examples are to be seen at Sycharth (p. 51) (plate 1) and Cardiff (p.110) (plate 13). They vary in size, and would have supported a timber palisade around the perimeter and probably a tower in the middle. Only a few motte summits have been excavated scientifically, so it cannot be said categorically that every motte had a tower. In some cases there may have been just a simple watchtower, perhaps alongside domestic accommodation. The majority of mottes had one or more baileys, defended courtyards where a range of buildings would have stood. The ringwork was an embanked and palisaded enclosure, usually circular, to which a bailey might be attached, and was a form much favoured by the Normans in central southern Glamorgan, where the subsoil was too shallow to allow for the construction of mottes. Although not included in the gazetteer, the ringwork of Caer Penrhos, Llanrhystud in Cardiganshire, is a good example of this type of castle (plate 2). It was built within a prehistoric hillfort, and is probably the castle that was founded in 1149 by Cadwaladr ap Gruffudd ap Cynan.

until the early twelfth century. In the Welsh Chronicles of the Welsh Princes (*Brut y Tywysogyon*) there is a reference under the year 1111 to a Welsh lord killed near Welshpool in Montgomeryshire whilst planning to build a castle. In 1116 the same source mentions a small castle near Cymer, not far from Dolgellau, built by a Welshman and destroyed by rival Welsh lords; traces of the castle's mound, or motte, survive under a later folly. One of the finest castle earthworks to be seen in Wales is the motte and bailey of Tomen y Rhodwydd in Denbighshire, built in 1149 by one of the great Welsh princes of the twelfth century, Owain Gwynedd.

Although we cannot be certain what the first castle of Chepstow (*c.*1070) looked like, the imposing great tower is the earliest masonry structure of a castle in Wales, built on the orders of William I, probably at the time of the king's visit to south Wales in 1081 (plate 15). At the same time, the king ordered the construction of the great motte within the walls of the Roman fort at Cardiff, presumably with a timber palisade and tower on its summit. Few castles in England and Wales have masonry as early as that at Chepstow – earth and timber was the norm. This was to change from the first half of the twelfth century, as the Normans established a greater footing, particularly in south Wales.

In lowland Glamorgan, for example, Robert fitz Hamon and those who owed him allegiance moved west from Gloucester to extend their control to the banks of the river Ogmore. Three castles built as a result of this drive west are to be seen at Ogmore, Coity and Newcastle. At the former two their origin is clear, castle ringworks with timber defences and internal buildings, but in the first half of the twelfth century they underwent a transformation. Coity's timber palisade was replaced by a stone curtain wall, whilst a keep or great tower was built on the line of the curtain, overlooking the approach to the main entrance. A similarly positioned keep is to be seen at Ogmore, although at this castle the timber palisade remained until the early thirteenth century. Small keeps in a comparable 'offensive' position can be found at several castles in south Wales, other examples being White Castle and Usk in Monmouthshire.

Another form of Norman keep is known as the shell keep, where a stone wall replaced a timber palisade around the edge of the summit of a motte. The best example is at Cardiff (plate 13), whilst others can be seen at Tretower in Breconshire and Wiston in Pembrokeshire.

The entrances to castles were often simple gateways – arched openings in the curtain in the lee of main towers, or sometimes through a square gate tower – but about 1190 an innovative gatehouse with twin rounded towers was built by William Marshal as the outer entrance to his castle at Chepstow (plate 15). This form of gatehouse, which incorporated apartments on the upper levels, is to be seen at most of the major castles in England and Wales from the thirteenth century onwards, although in some cases the towers may be square or polygonal. In terms of both military and domestic sophistication, the peak of gatehouse construction is represented by some of the castles built by Edward I and his lords following the conquest of Wales in the war of 1282–3, particularly Caernarfon, Denbigh (plate 7) and Harlech (plate 6), not forgetting Beaumaris of 1295. Good examples are also to be seen at Montgomery (Montgomeryshire), Caerphilly (Glamorgan) and Carreg Cennen (Carmarthenshire), whilst fine examples from the later Middle Ages are also to be found in Carmarthenshire, at Kidwelly (plate 11) and Carmarthen itself, and in the mid-fifteenth century at Raglan (Monmouthshire) (plate 16).

From the early thirteenth century onwards, at the same time as gatehouses became more sophisticated, we see the introduction of rounded or D-shaped mural towers projecting from curtain walls. They were usually equipped with arrowslits. It is rare to find twelfth-century mural towers in British castles, although square or rectangular examples can be seen in the castles of Dover in Kent and Orford in Suffolk, but nearer home, at the Newcastle in Bridgend, there are two Norman mural towers still standing in a castle relatively unaltered since the twelfth century.

In many cases the mural towers were provided with basic amenities such as fireplaces and latrines on one or more floors, so that the towers could be used for accommodation as well as defence. Again Chepstow (plate 15) provides some of the best examples of these developments in the first half of the thirteenth century, as do the three castles of Grosmont, Skenfrith and White (Monmouthshire), whilst in the second half of the century there are Caerphilly, Kidwelly (plate 11), Laugharne (Carmarthenshire) and Pembroke, as well as the Edwardian castles in north Wales.

Only two Welsh princely castles incorporate twin-towered gatehouses: Llywelyn ab Iorwerth's Cricieth in Caernarfonshire (plate 5) and Dinas Brân, built by the lords of northern Powys above Llangollen in Denbighshire. The gates at these two castles are not as sophisticated as those built by the Welsh Marcher lords, but where we do see Welsh building on a par with the English is in the great circular keeps of the first half of the thirteenth century. This form of great tower, although not common, is mainly found in south Wales, but there are examples in England and Scotland, with three in north Wales. The decision to build these circular towers, many on mottes, and with all-round vision from the battlements, may have been linked to the threat to the Marcher lords from the rise of the house of Gwynedd under Llywelyn the Great. Nevertheless, two castles in Carmarthenshire that were built by Welsh lords, Dinefwr and Dryslwyn, both have round keeps similar to the English manner (see figure 1), as does Dolbadarn.

A characteristic of several castles of the Welsh princes is the use of a very elongated D-shaped or apsidal tower, often along with rectangular towers; the only comparable 'English' version of such towers is the well tower at Montgomery as originally built in the 1220s. The best examples of apsidal towers are at Castell y Bere in Merioneth, overlooking the north and south approaches to the castle. The highest point of the castle, however, is occupied by a small rectangular tower.

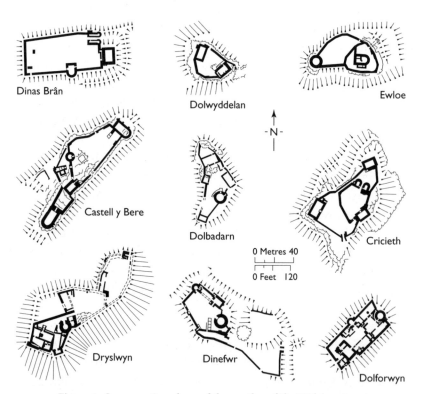

Figure 1: Comparative plans of the castles of the Welsh princes

The pinnacle of defensive sophistication was reached in those castles built by Edward I following the Welsh wars of 1277 and 1282–3. Apart from rebuilding Builth in Breconshire, the king's new castles were Aberystwyth (Cardiganshire), Flint and Rhuddlan (Flintshire), Caernarfon and Conwy (Caernarfonshire), Harlech (Merioneth), and the last in the sequence, Beaumaris (Anglesey), begun as a result of the revolt of Madog ap Llywelyn in 1294–5 (see p. 55). Of these castles, the latter four are quite remarkable, especially Caernarfon and Conwy with their town walls. They have few equals in Europe, and rightly they are

The construction of the castles of Edward I

Whatever one's views are of the Edwardian conquest of north Wales, from the point of view of building history, the construction of the castles is one of the greatest achievements of the Middle Ages. This achievement is made all the clearer because of the surviving documentation held by The National Archives, Kew. Although many documents have been lost over the years, and much was destroyed when the Welsh sacked the town and castle of Caernarfon in 1294, a vast amount survives and has been detailed in *The History of the King's Works* (see Further Reading, p. 156). The costs of the Edwardian castles detailed in King's Works need to be multiplied by 440 to arrive as near as possible at the modern equivalent.

The large numbers of men conscripted, especially for the castles built from 1283 (Caernarfon, Conwy and Harlech), are detailed in the surviving accounts. For example, we know that Shropshire and Staffordshire provided a certain number of carpenters (fifteen), diggers (forty) and masons (thirty), as well as woodcutters, and virtually every county in England had to raise a specific quantity of workmen. These craftsmen were assembled either at Bristol or Chester before being dispersed round the various castles. With the building season usually running from April to November, it was only by having a well-administered and large workforce that the castles could have been built so quickly.

Much has been made of the Savoyard connection with Edward's castles. In overall charge for much of the time was Master James of St George from Savoy, an area now incorporated into parts of France, Italy and Switzerland, and there were other Savoyard workmen. Recent scholarship has suggested that Master James should be best seen as having overall responsibility for the works, rather than as the actual designer of the strongholds, but there are architectural features at several of the castles – windows, arches and latrines – that have links with Savoy.

now inscribed on the World Heritage List. Caerphilly in the south, with its powerful twin-towered gatehouses, mural towers and ranges of additional defences, anticipates to some extent Edward's castles in the north, as does Kidwelly's inner ward or courtyard defences. At the same time as Edward was building his ring of fortresses around Gwynedd, several of his lords established castles in the north, for example, Chirk and Denbigh (Denbighshire).

Castle walls and towers provided powerful defences but, surprisingly, castles were rarely threatened during military operations. On only a few occasions, for example, during the Owain Glyndŵr uprising in the first decade of the fifteenth century and the civil war between king and Parliament in the 1640s, were major sieges of Welsh castles a significant feature of campaigns. Castle garrisons and supporting staff were often small in number, unless visited by their lords, and when Caernarfon was besieged in 1403 and 1404 by the Welsh, supported by the French, there were only a handful of soldiers to resist successfully, albeit aided by the townspeople.

However, castles were not just about fortifications. The castle as residence was equally important, so increasing attention was paid to the accommodation and supporting facilities. The first building phases at Caerphilly spanned the period 1268–71 and saw the construction of the great hall and private apartments. Soon after, around 1277–90, a massive kitchen range consisting of two towers was added against the hall. At Kidwelly a new hall, kitchen and magnificent chapel tower were built by about 1300, whilst at Chepstow Roger Bigod, fifth earl of Norfolk, transformed the lower courtyard or bailey in the late thirteenth century, building the huge Marten's Tower, with fine rooms and its own chapel, perhaps in anticipation of another visit by his king, Across the courtyard from Marten's Tower, Bigod built a new hall and a handsome kitchen range, the two being divided from each other by service rooms. In the south-west, in Pembrokeshire, we find grand suites of accommodation at Carew and Pembroke, whilst in the north the largely unaltered royal apartments in the inner ward of Conwy are considered to be the best surviving examples in England and Wales. At both Conwy and Beaumaris there was a fine chapel linked to the royal apartments.

Besides the kitchen, other service rooms that would be found in most castle households would have included butteries and pantries, as well as brewhouses for beer – little water would have been drunk. The buttery was a storeroom placed close to the hall where beers and wines would have been housed, while the pantry, also placed near the hall, housed eating implements and was the room from where the issue of bread for the table was controlled.

Nor were castles grey, forbidding buildings with bare stone walls. Many a castle had a limewashed exterior, so that it appeared white, hence the White Tower of London and, nearer home, White Castle in Monmouthshire. The interiors were often plastered, painted and decorated, and good, but fragmentary, examples can be seen at Chepstow and also at Manorbier in Pembrokeshire.

Several castles were set in their own parkland in which hunting could be enjoyed, such as Raglan, and many had gardens, and not just outside their walls. There was a garden for Edward I's queen adjacent to the royal apartments at Conwy, whilst we know from documentary evidence that there was a garden inside Kidwelly Castle. Castles and their designed landscapes have been a feature of recent innovative research of a number of castle and manorial studies.

In terms of castle building, the peak was reached by the late thirteenth century, and few new castles were built after that date, although others continued to be improved. An example of a new castle, although it was probably never completed, is Newport in Monmouthshire, with its handsome frontage overlooking the river Usk, built in the fourteenth century, and further enhanced in the fifteenth century. A castle that underwent major improvement in the 1300s was Caldicot, with a grander gatehouse built to mark the main entrance, with a new hall alongside; a similar rebuilding also occurred at Coity in Glamorgan in the same period. At the end of the fourteenth century one of the great gatehouses in Wales was begun, to replace an earlier gate at the main entrance to Kidwelly, for the castle had become the administrative headquarters of the Duchy of Lancaster's estates in south-west Wales. As well as providing a fine residence for the constable, it contained an office for duchy officials on the ground floor, set into which was a strongroom for valuables.

The greatest late medieval castle in England and Wales is without doubt Raglan, built from the 1430s to the 1460s. What we see there today is not an 'improvement' but a totally new fortress-palace that replaced the original castle and later manor house. Its high-quality carved masonry, handsome domestic ranges and fortified appearance with great tower and gatehouses signalled the rise, albeit short lived, of a relatively obscure Monmouthshire gentry family. Raglan's magnificent keep reminds us that, although the age of the keeps in England and Wales was in the twelfth and early thirteenth centuries, great towers continued to be built throughout the Middle Ages.

The close of the Middle Ages and the accession of the Tudor dynasty with King Henry VII (1485–1509) did not spell the end of many of our castles. The gazetteer entries show that a number, such as Carew (p. 62) and Raglan (p. 134), underwent improvements in the sixteenth and seventeenth centuries, and several saw military activity in the civil wars of the 1640s. The book concludes with a chapter on the 'aftermath' of medieval castle building, with a brief look at some 'castles' of the more modern period.

The gazetteer of sites

In the gazetteer of sites in the following chapters every entry is accompanied by Ordnance Survey map details and a grid reference. Entries will also indicate whether a castle is in the care of Cadw, the National Trust or another body, if known, whether there is an entry charge and whether a guidebook is known to be available. The county names are those of the historic counties.

For details regarding access and hours of opening, visitors, especially those with problems of mobility, are advised to consult the relevant websites; for example, *www.cadw.wales.gov.uk* and *www. nationaltrust.org.uk*. Many of Cadw's sites have free access and no custodian on site; guidebooks for these castles, when available, can be obtained from nearby staffed sites or through mail order (Cadw, Plas Carew, Unit 5/7 Cefn Coed, Parc Nantgarw, Cardiff CF15 7QQ).

Unless ownership/guardianship is specified, the sites are generally accessible on open land or are close to and viewable from roads and footpaths. If in doubt, always seek permission to visit a site.

2

The North-West

(Anglesey, Caernarfonshire, Merioneth)

Aberlleiniog motte, Llangoed, Anglesey

Ordnance Survey: Landranger 114, 115. *SH: 616 794.* Menter Môn.

This fine motte, acquired in 2004 by Menter Môn, the rural
development agency for Anglesey, lies close to Penmon, and is
accessible via various public footpaths. As work is ongoing on the site
at the time of writing, Menter Môn should be contacted before visiting
(telephone: 01248 725700).

The castle was one of the first to be built in Wales, the motte being
raised by Hugh d'Avranches, earl of Chester, in the late eleventh
century. Not long after, it was taken by the Welsh under Gruffudd ap
Cynan in 1094, a year of Welsh resurgence in the north against the
Normans. A civil war fort of the 1640s was later erected by the royalists,
and there is some evidence for this still. However, the masonry is
probably to be associated with an eighteenth-century folly, reused in
the Second World War as a Home Guard position.

Beaumaris Castle, Anglesey

Ordnance Survey: Landranger 114, 115. *SH: 607 763.*
Guidebook. Entry charge. Cadw. World Heritage Site.

Situated at the east end of the town, this was King Edward I's final castle
in Wales (figure 2). Although construction did not begin until 1295,
following the suppression of the 1294–5 Welsh uprising of Madog ap
Llywelyn (see p. 55), most of what can be seen today was constructed
in a year, a remarkable achievement, even by the standards of the king's
works elsewhere in Wales. Some works were undertaken from the early
1300s, mainly to finish the outer defences but, in spite of this,

Beaumaris was not completed when work finished in the 1330s, apart from the actual curtain walls. Much of the south gatehouse remains unfinished, as do the upper storeys of the inner ward and the inner half of the north gatehouse. We can obtain a real idea of the intended height

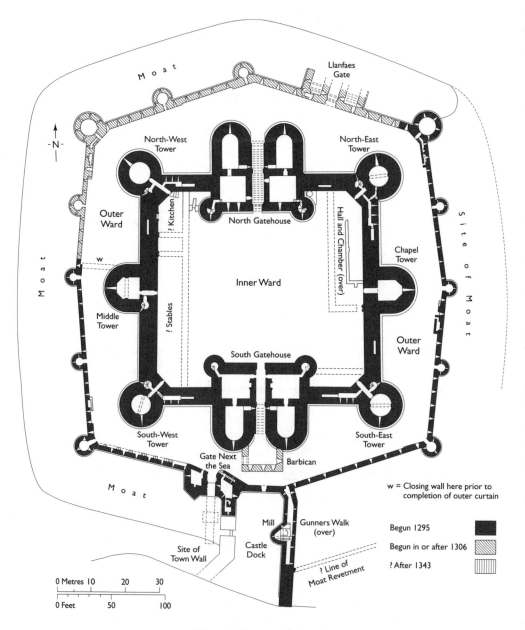

Figure 2: Beaumaris Castle

of the castle only by looking at the front of the north gatehouse, but even here the battlements are missing. The total cost of the castle was around £14,500 in the money of the day, with over £6,000 spent in the first six months (see p. 7).

From the fifteenth century the history of the castle was one of deterioration. It was held for the king in the civil war of the 1640s before surrendering to Parliament in 1646. Parts of the castle appear to have been dismantled at the time of the Restoration of King Charles II in 1660, and thereafter it became a picturesque ruin that continued to crumble, like many a castle, until conservation began in the twentieth century after it had passed into state care.

Beaumaris is a concentric castle (see p. 124), its taller inner ward towers overlooking the ring of outer defences. Crossing the moat, which once totally surrounded the castle, immediately on the right are the foundations of the town walls, whilst beyond is the castle dock in which small vessels would have berthed. The dock was protected by a flanking wall, the upper part of which is known as the Gunner's Walk. A projecting tower in this wall housed what was either a watermill or sluices to control the water in and out of the moat.

The outer gate is the Gate next the Sea, which would have been protected by a drawbridge, murder slots or machicolations, through which missiles could be dropped, and wooden gates. The gate has a number of small chambers, fireplaces and a latrine for the castle guards, and the outer curtain wall on either side could be accessed from within the gatehouse or from steps nearby.

The outer curtain has a number of small towers with arrowslits, with a larger example at both the north-west and north-east corners. These larger towers were designed for accommodation as well as defence, and had their own latrines, whilst a number of communal latrines are located elsewhere in the outer curtain. The plentiful provision of latrines is one of the remarkable features of this castle (see below); they are referred to as 'petites mesones' (little houses) in the fourteenth-century accounts. On the north-east side of the outer curtain stands the Llanfaes Gate, left unfinished in the 1330s, the twin towers lacking their rounded fronts.

Because the south gatehouse was never finished, and its three portcullises were never installed, a small barbican or outer defence was built against the face of the gate, to make it harder for an attacker who had reached the outer ward to gain access to the heart of the castle. The inner ward in all castles would have been full of buildings, and Beaumaris was no exception, but little can be seen today. Passing through the south gatehouse with its guard chambers and porters' lodges into the inner ward, the site of the hall and royal chambers lay to the right, between the north-east and chapel towers; more of a temporary structure must have been built where the hall range was planned, as a roofline cuts across the upper part of both its fireplaces. The area against the curtain on the left was probably the location of the stables, unless these were in the outer ward, the kitchen and other service buildings.

The rear of the north gatehouse was completed up to the first-floor hall and chamber, both with fireplaces, and lit by a row of five windows. If completed there would have been similar accommodation above, also well lit. The window on the left may have contained a doorway for an external staircase from the courtyard, but the stair turrets also linked all levels.

A network of passages within the curtain walls linked all the towers, and in the towers themselves arches to support floors can be seen, as well a number of fireplaces and windows. The basements of the towers just had a sloping vent for light, and would have been used for storage or even prisons. The central tower on the east side was the most elaborate as it housed the vaulted chapel on the first floor, lit by five lancet windows, with blind arcading decorating the wall beneath (plate 3). On each side of the chapel is a small elevated viewing chamber, from which the king and members of his household could view in privacy Mass being said in the chapel itself.

The mural passages also gave access to a number of latrines, but the best view of these is from the wall-walk. There are two pairs in each of the long curtain walls on the east and west sides, whilst in each of the short stretches on either side of the gatehouses there is a single pair. A ventilation shaft runs between each pair of latrines, and the steps down to each latrine still exist, as does the evidence for doorways and the latrine seats. The latrine pits were 'flushed' by the tide entering and exiting the moat.

Caernarfon Castle and town walls, Caernarfonshire

Ordnance Survey: Landranger 115. *SH: 477 626.*

Entry charge. Guidebook. Cadw. World Heritage Site.

Caernarfon Castle (figure 3), built from 1283 through to the 1320s, but like Beaumaris never completed to the original plan, is the most remarkable of King Edward I's castles in north Wales. The massive polygonal towers, with contrasting bands of stonework, have often been compared with the fifth-century walls of Constantinople (modern Istanbul), but it is now thought that it is more likely that Roman remains in Britain were the inspiration, such as those in York, particularly the Multangular Tower. Caernarfon incorporated the site of a late eleventh-century motte-and-bailey castle built by the Normans, the motte still being evident in nineteenth-century photographs.

Begun in 1283, the castle was to become the centre of administration in the north for the English Crown. The initial phase of construction, which ran to 1292, concentrated on the south or quay side of the castle, from the Eagle Tower to the North-east Tower, and the town walls to the north. Only the lower courses of the north side of the castle, including the King's Gate, were raised initially, since that side was protected by a great ditch and also by the town walls. By 1292 some £12,000 had been spent, most of it in the first five years of construction, and by this date the town walls had been finished and most of the southern curtain wall and mural towers had been built up to a defensible level.

In 1294 the castle and town suffered disaster during the revolt of Madog ap Llywelyn, which spread through much of Wales (see p. 55). The town was taken, its walls being badly damaged, as was the castle, for its incomplete defences on the north side were not strong enough to keep the Welsh out. Following the suppression of the revolt instructions were given that by November 1295 the town walls were to have been repaired, which they duly were, and ahead of time. From February of the following year work resumed on the castle, and by 1301 almost £4,500 had been expended here, on the King's Gate, the Well and Granary towers on either side, as well as the intervening curtain wall. Apart from a break from 1301 to 1304, probably due to the king's war in Scotland, work continued at Caernarfon until at least 1330. The Eagle Tower was almost finished in 1317, having been raised to four storeys and surmounted by three turrets adorned with helmeted heads and at least one stone eagle. In 1320 the statue of King Edward II (1307–27) was added to the front of the King's Gate.

The observant will note once inside the castle that many areas were left incomplete, with stones known as toothing projecting from towers to provide bonding for walls that were never constructed. These are particularly evident on the North-east Tower. The back of the Queen's Gate is clearly unfinished and the King's Gate was not completed to plan, which is unfortunate as it would have been one of the most remarkable defensive structures of any castle.

Although the castle remained the centre of administration in the north, the fabric began to decay from the fifteenth century, and by 1620 only the Eagle Tower and the King's Gate remained roofed. In spite of being held for the king in the civil war of the 1640s, following the Restoration orders were given for the total demolition of the castle and the town walls. Fortunately this did not happen, but the castle continued to deteriorate until the nineteenth century, when various programmes of restoration were embarked upon, notably under Sir Llewelyn Turner, the deputy-constable from 1870 until his death in 1903.

Caernarfon has always been the property of the Crown, but from 1908 its maintenance was passed to the state, and the emphasis shifted to conservation rather than restoration.

In the Middle Ages there were several potential entrances into the castle. The King's Gate and the Queen's Gate were the main ways in, but a doorway in the basement of the Eagle Tower was used by those arriving by water, and a small doorway or postern by the Chamberlain Tower led up and into one end of the hall. Goods arriving at the castle by water could also be brought up the ditch and through a well-defended doorway set into the Well Tower.

Entering the King's Gate, originally reached by passing over a drawbridge, you pass through a passage defended by guard chambers, doorways, arrowslits, portcullises and murder holes in the roof. Beyond the passage one is out in the open, between the upper and lower wards. However, the original plan would have seen the gate passage continue, and to reach the lower ward, in which lay the hall and kitchens, it would have been necessary to negotiate a further series of obstacles, including portcullises. A notable feature at first-floor level in the gate is the series of triple openings for archers in the wall-passages, each group served by only one slit on the external face of the castle. So, any attacker viewing the outside of the gate would be unaware of the fact that behind each slit there could be up to three archers, not one. This feature is also to be seen on the second floor and in the curtain wall between the gate and the North-east Tower. A chapel, one of many in the castle, is on the first floor, and above it lay the hall, lit by handsome windows.

A number of the mural towers hold exhibitions or form part of the regimental museum of the Royal Welch Fusiliers, and on the south side wall-passages lead one along the curtain walls and the outer sides of the upper levels of the towers themselves, so that anyone could pass from one end of the castle to the other, from the Queen's Tower to the Queen's Gate, without having to pass through the rooms in each tower.

Caernarfon is a castle with many fine towers. Most have several chambers and are generally well provided with latrines, and in several there are small rooms which may well have been chapels. The finest tower, without equal, is the Eagle Tower, designed initially to provide accommodation for the king's senior representative in north Wales, Sir Otto de Grandson. It too has three storeys or floors over a basement,

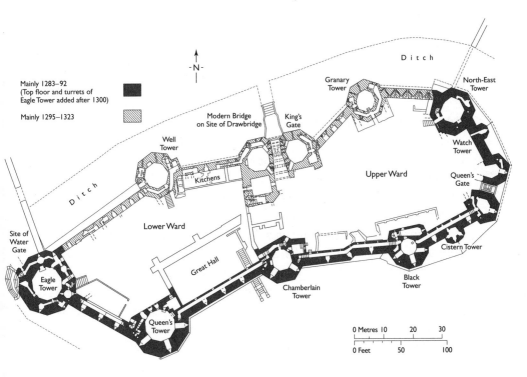

Figure 3: Caernarfon Castle

like the castle's other towers, but it is distinguished from the others by its size, three turrets and numerous wall or mural chambers within the thickness of its massive external wall. The basement can be entered from the lower ward as well as from the outside; a passage off the basement leads to what was originally intended to be the Water Gate, through which supplies would have passed on their way to the Well Tower. The ground floor is also reached from a doorway off the lower ward, and one of the mural chambers off the main room was originally a small octagonal chapel. The first floor was the main room until the upper storey was finally added, and now contains a theatre.

The second floor is well lit, the window embrasures having seats; there is a large fireplace, and one of the mural chambers may have been a small privy kitchen. The main stair continues from this level to the roof and its turrets.

Other points of interest in the castle include the Cistern Tower, which had a stone tank designed to hold rainwater; the water could be channelled towards the Queen's Gate. The Watch Tower, on the other side of the Queen's Gate, has grooves cut into its battlements in which wooden shutters would have been hung as protection for those manning the position.

Apart from the chambers in the towers, there is little evidence for the domestic buildings in the castle. The Great Hall, for example, between the Queen's Tower and the Chamberlain Tower survives only at foundation level. However, opposite the hall lie the kitchens and, although they may never have been completed, like so much else in the castle, enough remains to make them worth examining; how they worked is well explained in the guidebook. The castle's well is located in the adjacent tower, and from it water could be piped into the kitchens. The most obvious feature of the range is the setting for two cauldrons in which meat would have been boiled.

Associated with the castle was the small town occupied by English burgesses. It was defended by a curtain wall with eight towers, one circular and the remainder open backed, and two twin-towered gatehouses, together with two postern doorways. The walls can be viewed from the outside, as well partly from within the town. In many cases the battlements are modern rebuilds, but the mural tower north of the East Gate stands to its original height.

Castell Prysor, Merioneth

Ordnance Survey: Landranger 124. *SH: 758 369.* Private.

This castle mound, on private land, is visible from the side of the A4212, the Trawsfynydd to Bala road. It consists of a knoll of rock, heightened and also revetted in masonry, commanding the west end of the valley. It may have been constructed in the late twelfth century, although the only date possibly associated with it is 1284, when King Edward I sent a letter from 'Pressor' in July of that year. The Welsh antiquary Thomas Pennant mentioned in the late eighteenth century that, apart from traces of buildings about the castle, there was a wall around the mound's summit and a possible round tower. If the tower was circular, then a date in the first half of the thirteenth century is likely. The masonry revetment was originally mortared. There are traces of rectangular buildings to the north-west and north-east, and it has been suggested that at Prysor we have a Welsh castle and a *llys*, or royal residence.

Castell y Bere, Merioneth

Ordnance Survey: Landranger 124. *SH: 669 086.*
Guidebook. Cadw.

Carreg Cennen and Harlech may look dramatic, perched as they are high up on rocky crags, but few castles can rival the spectacular position of Castell y Bere, a now very ruinous castle built on a large outcrop of rock which stands like an island in the southern foothills of Cadair Idris (figure 1).

Llywelyn ab Iorwerth built a castle here in 1221, in a position to control the route from Tywyn to the south up to Dolgellau. Its position here meant that in King Edward I's second campaign in Wales its capture in April 1283 was a necessity. For a short period the English garrisoned it, with a small town being founded. Various building works were undertaken in the 1280s and 1290s, but it may have been abandoned soon after the Welsh uprising of 1294–5. The masonry remains indicate the full extent of the plan, but only parts of the castle stand to any great height.

Most of the castle is Llywelyn's, although the thick walling between the middle tower, at the highest point of the castle, and the large apsidal south tower is of English build. It is possible that part of the defensive arrangements at the entrance may also be English rebuild, but the fragmentary nature of the masonry makes it impossible to be certain. A quantity of finely carved masonry, from the first half of the thirteenth century, was found when the castle was cleared in 1851 and is now in the National Museum of Wales in Cardiff.

The castle sits within natural defences, strengthened to the north and south by rock-cut ditches. Two ditches have to be crossed before the entrance is reached. A drawbridge would have given access to the gate-passage, overlooked by a square tower or guardroom, and then on over another bridge to the inner gate, which sits next to the round tower. The middle tower, or small keep, and the south tower also overlook the approaches to the entrance, making the whole arrangement one of the most sophisticated entrances to any castle of the Welsh princes.

Within the courtyard there are the footings of a number of buildings of uncertain date built against the curtain wall, and just inside the entrance is the well or cistern. The finest accommodation in this part of the castle was undoubtedly in the apsidal north tower. The main room was on the first floor, reached by a stone staircase, later rebuilt, and the pillar in the basement may have supported a central hearth on the floor above. The quality of the masonry found here suggests that this tower was Llywelyn's hall or chamber, perhaps with a chapel. Another fine apsidal tower was built at the southern end of the ridge, but how it was connected to the rest of the castle is not known, as the walling around the so-called ditch yard is of English build. This south tower, more substantial than that to the north, may date to the first half of the thirteenth century, but it could also have been added around the 1260s by Llywelyn ap Gruffudd. The main accommodation would also have been on the first floor. The basement has embrasures for slit windows, and a doorway and passage lead to a latrine that would have served both floors.

Conwy Castle and town walls, Caernarfonshire

Ordnance Survey: Landranger 115. *SH: 784 774.*
Entry charge. Guidebook. Cadw. World Heritage Site.

Few European medieval fortifications come close to rivalling the castle and town defences at Conwy (plate 4; figure 4). They were built following the second Welsh war of King Edward I, and what is truly remarkable is that it took only four years to build them, at a cost of about £15,000 (see p. 7).

King Edward chose a new site for his castle, the first castle in this area being on the twin peaks of Deganwy, across the estuary (see below). The establishment of the associated town resulted in the

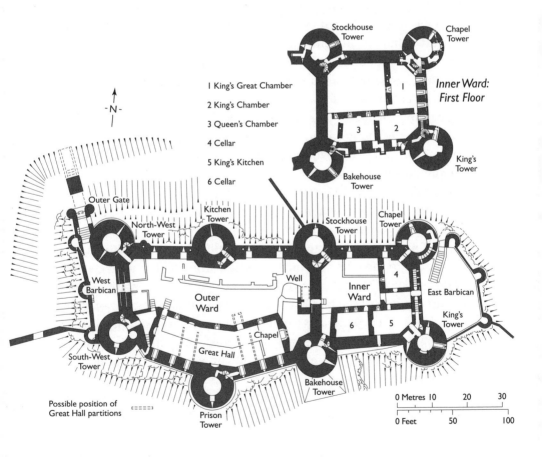

Figure 4: Conwy Castle

removal of the Cistercian monastery of Aberconwy to a new site some miles away, leaving the church to serve the new borough. In 1283–4 construction works focused on the castle's towers and the curtain walls between them to provide a perimeter that could be defended. It has been calculated that this work cost almost £6,000. Once these were virtually complete, the building of the internal buildings then commenced. The town walls were being constructed in 1285; the work was undertaken in several stages, but completed by 1286–7.

King Edward was at the castle in December/January 1294–5, during the Madog ap Llywelyn uprising, possibly the only time that he resided there. In the fourteenth century, repairs and new works were undertaken, due to the poor state of the various towers and buildings of the castle. For example, eight stone arches were inserted in the hall in 1346–7 as part of a new roof. In 1401 the castle was taken and held for three months by supporters of Owain Glyndŵr. Thereafter, little appears to have been done to maintain the castle, apart from repairs to both it and town walls in the reign of King Henry VIII (1509–47). Conwy was held for King Charles in the civil war of the 1640s, before being taken by Parliament's forces. Soon after, one of the castle's towers was deliberately slighted or damaged to make the castle less defensible, and following the Restoration of 1660 much of the reusable material such as ironwork and lead was stripped. In this way the castle became the ruined shell of today. Both the castle and town walls came into the care of the state in 1953, and a conservation programme began that continues to this day, enabling the visitor to explore the castle fully and to access most of the town walls.

The modern path up to the castle, leading from the visitor centre, zigzags up to the outer defence, or west barbican, that protected the main entrance. The path is overlooked by two of the great towers, and in the curtain wall can be seen the outlets for the latrines, one of which is still protected within its small curved masonry wall. It is worth pausing to examine the massive north-west tower that overlooks the entrance to the castle. Whilst small slits provided minimum light for rooms probably used for storage, wider rectangular windows, originally divided into two 'lights', indicate well-lit upper chambers for accommodation. On the face of this tower small square holes mark the position of the original scaffolding that spiralled round the tower, providing a ramp for the masons, rather in the fashion of a helter-skelter! There are also arrowslits in the main body of the tower, as well as at battlement level, and there still remains evidence for little finials on the merlons, the merlons being the 'teeth' of the battlements, either side of the gaps known as crenels. Many of these features are repeated on the other seven towers of the castle. One must also remember that the castle would originally have had a lime render on the outside, so that, when first built, the walls would have been gleaming white. Traces of this render can be detected in various parts of the castle.

As one turns up some steps to enter the barbican, over to the right is the site of the drawbridge as well as the stub of the ramp that marks the original entrance to the castle from the town. The entrance into the barbican was defended by a doorway and portcullis, whilst the barbican itself has three small towers or turrets overlooking the town; the town wall meets the castle's defences below the southernmost turret (the other side of the town wall runs from the Stockhouse Tower). Unlike King Edward's castles of Beaumaris, Caernarfon and Harlech, there was no room for a great gatehouse here, so the entrance was guarded by the two corner towers, whilst a line of arched murder holes or machicolations, through which missiles could be dropped, can be seen surmounting the wall that contains the doorway. The entrance passage, which would have had a portcullis and wooden doors, leads into the outer ward.

The outer ward contains the foundations of the stables and kitchen on the left; the latter adjoined the Kitchen Tower, the lower rooms of which would have served as kitchen storerooms. On the right side of the ward lies the hall range set over a cellar. The central part of the range, backing on to the Prison Tower, contained the hall, whilst at the west end there were two rooms, as the fireplaces indicate. To the east, beyond the hall, was a passage that originally was reached by a porch, forming the main entrance to the hall. That part of the building closest to the inner ward was the chapel, marked by a large window. The Prison Tower could be reached by passing through a doorway set in the side of a window embrasure at one end of the hall and, whilst the upper two rooms would have provided comfortable accommodation, as in the other towers, the lower two were clearly places of confinement, the basement being particularly grim – dark, with the only access being a rope lowered in the floor above through a trapdoor.

Approaching the inner ward, there is a well and the remains of the middle gate, which with its drawbridge would have controlled access to the king's and queen's private chambers. Those chambers in the inner ward were little altered once constructed, and they are considered to be the best surviving examples of medieval royal accommodation in England and Wales, even in their roofless state. On entering the inner ward the queen's chamber was on the right, with the king's chamber beyond it, both on the first floor. Running across the far side was the king's great chamber, again on the first floor. Timber stairways gave access to these apartments. Cellars lay below these rooms, apart from the king's chamber, for there lay the kitchen.

The inner ward is framed by four large towers, the western pair marking the junction between the two wards. The Bakehouse Tower was so named because of the large oven in the basement, with the upper floors containing accommodation for the queen's household. The Stockhouse Tower also would have been used for accommodation

Machicolations and hourding

One of the vulnerable areas of a fortification is the base of the walls, an area where attackers might place ladders to reach up to the battlements or attempt to undermine the defences. Although men on the battlements could lean out to try to counteract such activities, they would be exposed to the enemies' archers. The construction of machicolations and hourding was designed to assist the defenders by providing them with protection.

Machicolations are a series of arches, usually over the entrance to a castle, but also sometimes seen around the tops of towers, through which missiles could be dropped, or even water poured to douse any attempt to set fire to a castle's doors or outer portcullis. Raglan is a good example of a fifteenth-century castle with machicolations (plate 16), but the remains of what may be the earliest example can be seen at the entrance to the outer ward of Conwy Castle (p. 23).

Hourding provided even more protection to a garrison, for it was a roofed timber structure projecting beyond the battlements of a keep, mural tower or curtain wall. Although the holes for the horizontal beams that supported hourding often survive, and are sometimes mistaken for drain holes (and, indeed, vice versa), no example has survived the from Middle Ages in Britain. However, at Caerphilly Castle (p. 100) there is a section of hourding that has been reconstructed along the north-west section of the inner curtain wall.

and storage, although stocks and manacles in the tower in the early sixteenth century suggest that prisoners were also housed here at that time. To the east, the King's Tower would have accommodated the officials who served the king and queen in their chambers, as well as the staff who controlled who and what entered and left the kitchen, and other matters.

The Chapel Tower was just that; it housed an elaborate chapel on the first floor which, like Beaumaris, was provided with a small overlooking chamber from which the king could observe the Mass in privacy. This watching chamber was reached from the king's great chamber. Of the small rooms on either side of the chapel, one would have been the vestry, containing the vestments of the priests, while the other would have been the sacristy, a room in which the communion vessels were stored when not in use.

At the far end of the inner ward is a passage through to the east barbican. Approaching this doorway stairs can be seen on either side, leading up to the two eastern towers. The approach to the entrance to the inner ward from the barbican also had murder holes, whilst below them can be seen the fine windows that lit the first-floor chambers. The king and queen could reach their accommodation in relative privacy by water, for below one side of the barbican originally lay the water gate, with stairs leading up from it, and no doubt goods for the royal kitchen would have entered this way. The barbican is strengthened with three turrets and originally contained a garden.

The castle's battlements can be reached from six of the great towers, and provide superb views of not just the surrounding land- and seascape, but also the interior of the castle. Although it is possible to walk freely around the battlements, in the Middle Ages doors would have controlled access at this level between the inner and outer wards.

Town walls survive in many of our urban centres, but the high degree of survival in an almost unaltered state make those at Conwy almost unique, and in only a few instances have roads and rail broken through the original fabric. Much of circuit can be seen from outside the walls, and long stretches of the battlemented wall-walk are freely accessible.

The walls have twenty-one towers, two postern gates and three twin-towered gatehouses; there was also a tower at the end of the spur wall or breakwater at the opposite end of the quay to the castle, but this has long since disappeared. The majority of the towers are D-shaped and were never roofed. Arrowslits are visible in the upper levels, and in the battlemented wall-walks, whilst at the rear of each tower there was originally timber planking rather than a stone wall-walk. Should an enemy gain access to one part of the circuit, the removal of the planking would prevent him from reaching other parts of the defences.

The stretch of walls along the quay, with the Lower Gate and the first four towers, is the least impressive section, as modern buildings encroach on the walls. The best section is from the tower (numbered 5 in the Cadw guidebook) and postern gate at the end of the quay along the western side of the walls up to the highest point of the circuit, the round tower 13. Tower 10 had a road pushed through it in the nineteenth century, whilst the crack in tower 11 is due to the railway tunnel that runs below. Set just below tower 13 to the south-east is the Upper Gate, with the remains of its barbican; the modern road here is considerably lower than its medieval equivalent. This section of the circuit, between towers 13 and 15, has one of the finest sections of battlemented walling.

The windows in the town wall beyond tower 15, along with the next tower (16), mark the site of a building known as Llywelyn's Hall, a small residential block with a chapel, used by the future King Edward II as prince of Wales in the early 1300s. In 1316 the hall was dismantled and re-erected in Caernarfon Castle as a storehouse.

Beyond the railway line is the Mill Gate, so named from the medieval mill that stood nearby. The gate is unusual in that one tower is rounded and the other D-shaped. A unique feature of the walls here is the line of twelve projecting latrines between the gatehouse and tower 18, providing necessary relief for the king's officials based inside the walls. The walls with the final three towers then continue up to the castle.

Cricieth Castle, Caernarfonshire

Ordnance Survey: Landranger 123. *SH: 499 376.*
Entry charge. Guidebook. Cadw.

Of all the native Welsh castles, Cricieth (plate 5; figure 1) is one of the finest surviving examples, and is unusual for having a twin-towered gatehouse; this is almost unique amongst the castles of the Welsh princes, although there is a poorer example at Dinas Brân, Denbighshire (p. 40). The castle is set on a great rock and has clear views of the adjacent coast, so it is no surprise that King Edward I made use of it following his conquest of north Wales in 1282–3; the king's new castle of Harlech (p. 35) is clearly visible from Cricieth.

The first reference to a castle here is in 1239, when Llywelyn ab Iorwerth imprisoned members of his family in it, and the inner ward with its sophisticated twin-towered gatehouse, together with the rectangular south-east tower (much rebuilt by Edward I), dates to this period. A gatehouse comparable in date and form is that at Beeston Castle, Cheshire, built by Ranulph de Blundeville, whose nephew and heir, John le Scot, had married a daughter of Llywelyn.

The castle was considerably enlarged from the later 1250s by Llywelyn ap Gruffudd to the north and south-west, with a curtain wall and two further rectangular towers enveloping his grandfather's stronghold on three sides. A gateway on the south side of the new curtain wall became the main entrance. From 1283 some £500 was spent on the castle by King Edward I, a considerable sum, but the accounts do not specify what was done. However, it is clear that, besides the work on the south-east tower, the gatehouse was heightened, a flight of steps was added against the north tower and improvements were made to the outer gate. Further work under King Edward II (1307–27) cost over £250; the gatehouse was heightened again and repairs were made to the towers and internal buildings. The castle remained in English hands until about 1404, when it was surrendered to Owain Glyndŵr and then destroyed.

From the visitor centre one passes the remains of the outer and inner banks, with a ditch between. When the castle was first built a path must have led to the inner ward gatehouse, but following the building of the outer gate around 1260, the approach led along the main seaward side of the castle, although this has since been quarried away. The modern route leads through the remains of the outer curtain, provided with arrowslits, which connected the south-west and north towers. The main building in the outer ward is the rectangular south-west tower, on one side of which are the remains of the late thirteenth-century staircase, as well as foundations of a building of unknown date. This tower as built by Llywelyn ap Gruffudd consisted of a first-floor hall over a basement, but it may have been heightened by Edward I by the addition of a second storey. Also dating to the Edwardian period is the entrance to the basement, flanked by slit windows. One other feature of interest in the outer ward is the small water cistern built up against the south-east tower and the doorway into the inner ward; still to be seen is the stone channel which would have housed a lead pipe.

A narrow passage connects the northern and southern parts of the outer ward. Originally covered by a lean-to or pent roof, it runs along the north side of the inner ward, passing the arched base of the latrine chute of the inner gatehouse. The walls of the north tower are at the level of the basement, but there would have been an upper storey, on

Llywelyn ab Iorwerth (c.1173–1240) and Llywelyn ap Gruffudd (d.1282)

These two men dominated Wales in the thirteenth century and at the height of their powers were an ever-present threat to the English kings and the lords of the Welsh March. Llywelyn ab Iorwerth has come down to us as Llywelyn Fawr (the Great), and although acclaimed by contemporaries only as the prince of Aberffraw and lord of Snowdon in north-west Wales his influence was felt on a much wider scale. He laid the foundation on which his grandson, Llywelyn ap Gruffudd, built, for a short period, an independent Wales, after King Henry III recognized him as prince of Wales in the Treaty of Montgomery in 1267. Both men took and destroyed many a castle in their campaigns, but were also great castle builders, including Cricieth and Dolforwyn (pp. 27, 54). Llywelyn ap Gruffudd's success lasted only ten years, for the Treaty of Aberconwy in November 1277, at the end of the first Welsh war of King Edward (p. 32), stripped him of most of powers, leaving him only Gwynedd. In the second Welsh war, he was surprised and killed in a battle or skirmish at Cilmeri, near Builth in Breconshire.

the roof of which a piece of artillery was mounted, thus leading to this tower being known as the Engine Tower. Four chutes visible on the outer face of the north-west side would have served a pair of latrines on the first floor and at battlement level.

The three phases of the twin-towered gatehouse are evident from the outer ward. Most of the masonry forms Llywelyn ab Iorwerth's gate, up to the line of horizontal sockets for a hourd or projecting timber gallery. The new battlements added by King Edward I were blocked in the third and final phase, in the early fourteenth century. The ground floor of the gatehouse has three arrowslits in both D-shaped towers. The gate passage is entered under a modern arch, just beyond which are the grooves for the portcullis. The passage floor is modern, but the spring-fed medieval cistern survives. To one side is the entrance to the guardroom or porter's lodge in the east tower; a similar room is to be seen in the west tower. The timbering of the first floor would have covered the rear of the passage. A suite of chambers, one possibly a chapel, was provided on the first and second floors of the gatehouse, both levels having access to latrines on the west side. The gatehouse now lacks its inner wall, but this would have contained fireplaces. At the rear of the eastern tower are the remains of three phases of staircases that led to the upper floors, and so on up to the battlements.

The south-east tower was entered from the inner ward. The basement of the tower was originally reached using a staircase from the floor above, but in about 1260 ground-floor access was created through a pair of doors, the outer being secured by a drawbar. The upper storey in the later thirteenth century was reached from the curtain wall, and, possibly, an external staircase from the inner ward. A single Edwardian latrine chute is visible on the north-east side, adjacent to four early thirteenth-century latrines reached by stairs from the inner ward.

Much of the inner ward's curtain wall stands to battlement level, with evidence for arrowslits, as well as drains to take rainwater from the roofs of the timber buildings that would have been arranged around the courtyard. To the south is a small doorway or postern, the back door into the first castle, but one that would have given access to the outer ward in the later thirteenth century.

Deganwy Castle, Caernarfonshire

Ordnance Survey: Landranger 115. *SH: 782 794.* **Open access.**

A public footpath between houses on York Road, Deganwy, leads up to the twin hills of the castle. This is the site of an early medieval Welsh stronghold that has a history stretching back to the sixth century. The Norman, Robert of Rhuddlan, established a castle here in the late eleventh century, a stronghold that came to be the centre of much dispute between Norman and Welsh in the following century. The Welsh destroyed the castle in the early thirteenth century before King John (1199–1216) could take it. Llywelyn ab Iorwerth rebuilt it from 1213, but little survives of this castle, or of that built in 1244–54 after the castle had been surrendered to King Henry III (1216–72). The king himself was present at its construction in 1245 and, although the new castle was unfinished by 1254, it cost about £10,000. The new work on the west hill was built in 1247–9. In 1250, Mansell's Tower was ordered to be heightened and roofed. The bailey between the hills was also to be walled in stone and provided with two twin-towered gatehouses, although this was completed only on the south. In 1263, Llywelyn ap Gruffudd took and systematically destroyed the castle, which is why there is so little to see today. A fine early thirteenth-century stone carving of a head, excavated in the 1960s and now in the National Museum of Wales in Cardiff, possibly represents Llywelyn ab Iorwerth himself; this is the only indication of the quality of the Welsh stronghold.

The core of the castle was known as the donjon and occupied the summit of the west hill, the bailey lying between it and the east hill on which stood the rounded Mansell's Tower. Most of the fragmentary remains belong to Henry III's castle. The main entrance lay on the south, where there are slight traces of a twin-towered gatehouse and, nearby, a prominent mass of fallen masonry from the demolition period. A gap and a stub of masonry mark the site of a northern entrance and on this side is a prominent bank and ditch; the bank may have been topped with just a timber palisade. At the south-east corner of the polygonal enclosure of the donjon are traces of a round tower overlooking the east inner entrance; adjoining the tower lay the hall. A further gateway lay on the south-west side of this hill. Remains of the curtain wall are evident on the north and west sides of the hill; the stone revetment on the north side is part of Llywelyn's castle.

Earthworks to the north may represent the remains of the mid-thirteenth-century English town.

Dolbadarn Castle, Caernarfonshire

Ordnance Survey: Landranger 115. *SH: 586 598.*
Guidebook. Cadw.

This castle (figure 1), the subject of some of the finest paintings produced by British landscape artists from the later eighteenth century, such as J. M. W. Turner and Richard Wilson, stands on a promontory that juts above the two lakes, Llyn Padarn and Llyn Peris. It is reached by a footpath over a stream from the nearby car park. It is one of the early thirteenth-century strongholds of Llywelyn ab Iorwerth (d.1240) and controlled access along the Llanberis Pass, one of the main routes through Snowdonia. The design of the main feature of the castle, the round keep, indicates Llywelyn's links through marriage with families of prominent English lords of the Welsh Marches. Three Welsh phases of development can be seen. The low drystone walls enclosing the promontory date from the beginning of the thirteenth century. The keep, with its mortared walls, was added about 1230. The curtain wall on the east side also dates from this time, but after the great tower had been built.

The foundations representing the south and west towers are of the first phase, and the other main building of this period was the hall at the promontory end of the site. Later in the thirteenth century the castle was considered strong enough for Llywelyn ap Gruffudd to confine his brother Owain in the main tower. The castle had fallen to Edward I by summer 1283, and the Crown accounts reveal that timber was removed in 1284 for the new works at Caernarfon. Nevertheless, the castle remained occupied as a royal centre, and repairs were undertaken in the early fourteenth century. The rectangular building to the north-east of the keep is clearly later, and dates from the English occupation. Thereafter, nothing is known of the castle's history.

The entrance to the castle today must mark the site of the original gateway, as the ground here is less precipitous than elsewhere around the castle. The two rectangular towers can never have stood particularly high, and both may simply have had a ground-floor chamber and a battlemented wall-walk. The hall would have dominated the enclosed courtyard, lying across the spur east to west; it had opposing doorways signifying a cross-passage at one end. A latrine lay outside to the north-east. In the east curtain wall there was a gate next to the footings of a small rectangular structure. A further entrance, reached externally by a short flight of steps, lies further south. It was here that the building added by the English Crown was constructed, utilizing the original curtain as its external wall. There may have been another tower at the north end of the site, or the two sides of the curtain wall may have met at an acute angle.

The round keep, its lowest courses of masonry sloped or battered, is approached by an external flight of steps of uncertain date. Originally, there may have been a timber staircase leading up to a porch. On the one side a projecting pent-roofed structure houses the latrines. The tower consisted of two floors or storeys over a basement, a rare feature in a castle of the Welsh princes, where most towers had only one main floor. Also unusual is the setting for a portcullis, unique in the round keeps of the English Marcher lords and other Welsh princes; in its raised position it sat within a window embrasure of the upper floor. The doorway, rebuilt in the last century, that leads into the

The Welsh wars of King Edward I

Llywelyn ap Gruffudd's failure to do homage to Edward, the new English king (1272–1307), and pay tribute, as agreed in the Treaty of Montgomery, was to lead to the first Welsh war (1277). With Edward's patience at end, an army of over 15,000 men moved against Llywelyn, and the English navy ensured that Anglesey, the granary of north-west Wales, was cut off from the Welsh. Llywelyn formerly surrendered in the Treaty of Aberconwy. The immediate catalyst of the second war, after a period of growing resentment against English officialdom, was Llywelyn's brother, Dafydd, who attacked Hawarden Castle in Flintshire in March 1282. Three armies advanced on the Welsh, from the south, mid Wales and the north, and the death of Llywelyn in December 1282 and the capture of a number of Welsh castles spelt the end of the main resistance. Dafydd finally was captured and executed in the summer of 1283. The end of both wars saw the construction of a number of new English castles (p. 7), and in March 1284 the Statute of Rhuddlan led to the creation of three shire counties in north-west Wales – Anglesey, Caernarvon and Merioneth.

first floor was secured by a drawbar, the socket for which remains on one side.

Sockets for the timber joists or beams mark the level of the first floor; originally a trapdoor in the floor would have given access to the basement. The only opening in the basement was a ventilation shaft on the east side. On the first floor a doorway leads into the latrine block, and on the south-east side is a window with seats in the embrasure. Close to this is the fireplace, and the top of its flue is a slit in the external face of the tower. The doorway to the north-west leads to a stair that spirals anticlockwise up to the upper floor, then on up clockwise to a landing at roof level and then up to the battlements. The stairs are lit by a series of small slit windows.

The upper floor was the main chamber, a room with four windows and a fireplace. A passage by the east window leads down to the latrine block. The only window without seating is that on the north, for it is here that the raised portcullis rested. The roof of the keep, set well below the wall-walk and battlements, is marked by a groove that runs all the way round the inner face of the tower, sockets and projecting stones or corbels taking the main and secondary timbers. The crenellated battlements have long since disappeared.

Dolwyddelan Castle, Caernarfonshire

Ordnance Survey: Landranger 115. *SH: 722 523.*
Entry charge. Guidebook. Cadw.

A path leading up from the car park and through the farmyard takes the visitor to Llywelyn ab Iorwerth's castle. Built some time after 1210, it was a replacement for Tomen Castell, a tree-covered mound just across the road, on the other side of the Lledr valley.

The castle (front cover; figure 1) is set on the slopes of Moel Siabod and dominates the valley and the line of the original road that lay to the west of the castle. The main tower or keep is the earliest part of the castle, but the construction of the curtain wall must be seen as part of the same plan, even though it butts against the tower. Although there is no evidence for any courtyard building dating to Llywelyn's time, at the north end of the later thirteenth-century west tower there is a latrine chamber that may have served an earlier tower or chamber block.

The castle was captured by the English during Edward I's Welsh war of 1282–3, garrisoned under the command of a Welshman and equipped with stone-throwing artillery and stone shot. The only reference to any new building work being undertaken relates to the construction of a lodging, and this has been taken to be the west tower, constructed soon after the castle's capture. The keep may have been heightened at the same time. In 1284, repairs were made to the lead and woodwork of various chambers, with further work undertaken in 1290–2.

By the early fourteenth century the castle may have been abandoned, but in the late fifteenth century it was leased to Maredudd ab Ieuan ap Robert, and to this period belongs the external staircase against the west tower leading up to the curtain wall. Between 1848 and 1850 the keep was restored; the battlements and the drains that project below them belong to this final phase, as do much of the north and south walls.

Where the precipitous natural slopes did not protect the castle, ditches were cut into the rock, to the east and west. The castle was entered through a simple doorway, adjacent to the west tower, and reached by a bridge spanning the ditch at this point. A further doorway is situated in the same stretch of curtain wall, and a small doorway or postern is set in a short section of curtain wall dating to the English occupation, north-east of the keep.

The two-storey west tower was built abutting the earlier curtain, the ground-floor chamber utilizing the earlier latrines, whilst a new set of latrines was built against the north-west corner of the curtain wall, to serve the first-floor chamber. That the first floor was the main chamber is shown by the large fireplace, and it must have been reached by an internal timber stair. To one side of the one window that remains on the upper floor a flight of steps led up to the roof level and the battlements. The late fifteenth-century external staircase butts against the south side of the tower.

The only other feature of the courtyard is the remains of an oven of unknown date, in the angle of the curtain and the south-west side of the keep.

The main tower as built by Llywelyn ab Iorwerth is the best surviving example of its type. Before its restoration, drawings show that the building stood to its upper walls, albeit roofless. The largely modern south wall includes a projection that houses a passage to the latrine, and against the west wall a flight of steps leads to the first-floor entrance. The landing outside the keep's doorway was covered by a porch or forebuilding, itself with a doorway and drawbar, whilst a pit within the porch provided an added defence; it would have had a bridge that could be moved or raised to prevent access to the keep.

Entry to the basement, a room lit by three small slits, must have been through a trapdoor at first-floor level. As first built, the roof over the main room on this level would have been lower than it is now, but the wide windows in the east and west walls are original and were provided with seats. The fireplace is in the east wall; it was restored in the nineteenth century, at which time the window above and to one side of it and another window in the upper west wall were also inserted. A doorway in the south-west corner opens into a passage leading to a latrine. The triangular outline of one gable of the original roof can be made out in the south wall. The north window in the east wall has a doorway to one side of the embrasure, and this leads to a staircase to the nineteenth-century roof and battlements.

Harlech Castle, Merioneth

Ordnance Survey: Landranger 124. *SH: 581 312.*
Entry charge. Guidebook. Cadw. World Heritage Site.

Although the sea that once lapped the west side of the rock on which the castle stands has long since retreated, Harlech still stands in a majestic position, the view from the south being one of the most popular photographic images of any castle (plate 6; figure 5). It was begun in the spring of 1283, once the forces of King Edward I had moved north following the capture of Castell y Bere in April of that year, and was completed by 1289, at a cost of about £8,000. Following the Madog ap Llywelyn revolt of 1294–5 the area immediately to the north, Castle Rock, was enclosed by a curtain wall, running from the Water Gate to the north-east tower, and in 1323–4 the main approach to the castle was strengthened by the addition of two towers.

Harlech's importance in Welsh history was assured with the revolt of Owain Glyndŵr, when it was captured, along with Aberystwyth, at the end of 1404. It became the main base of Glyndŵr and his family and was the location of one of his parliaments. Besieged from 1408 by the forces of Prince Henry, the future King Henry V (1413–22), it was taken early in 1409 with the use of cannon. It was held by the Lancastrians in the Wars of the Roses until taken in 1468 by the Yorkists under William Herbert of Raglan. The last Welsh castle to fall in those wars, that honour fell to it again in 1647 during the civil war, when Parliament's forces took it in March of that year.

Harlech is a beautifully symmetrical concentric castle, although the lower and thinner outer curtain wall has suffered in the sieges it underwent. The modern timber steps and bridges lead up to the main entrance over the remains of the two towers added in the 1320s. On this side and on the south the castle was also defended by a deep rock-cut ditch. The small gate to the outer ward consists of two solid turrets, and on either side are the stubs of the original curtain wall. Behind lies the massive twin-towered inner gate, complete up to its ruined battlements; the two windows between the towers, one above the

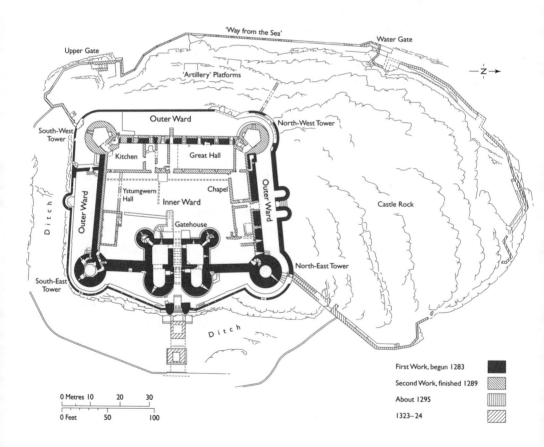

Figure 5: Harlech Castle

other, light chapels within. Anyone seeking access to the inner ward would have had to cross a drawbridge and then negotiate the obstacles at the main gate-passage: a massive door, two portcullises, another door and, at the far end of the passage, another portcullis and possibly another door. Arrowslits overlooked the passage, whilst on either side at the rear of the gate was a guardroom, in one of which are cannonballs which possibly date to one of the fifteenth-century sieges. A stair turret projects from the back of the gatehouse at both corners, reached from the guardrooms, and the stairs led up to the upper floors. An external staircase in the inner ward gave access to the first floor.

The great gatehouse provided handsome accommodation on the upper two floors for the constable of the castle or even for the king if he had visited. The twin towers themselves contained small chambers, probably bedrooms, and between them lay the chapels. On the inner side of the gatehouse each floor had two fine chambers with handsome windows overlooking the inner ward on the north, west and south sides, one room being larger than the other (perhaps a hall). The rooms had fireplaces, the flues from which ran up to linked chimneys, the remains of which are still visible above roof level. There was also access to a number of latrines.

At each corner of the inner ward is a large tower, with stairs leading up to the upper floors and the wall-walk. The two to the west were built in 1288–9, at the end of the main construction phase, at a time when the internal buildings were being added. The north-east and south-east towers have three floors, the upper polygonal rooms having fireplaces and windows, as well as adjacent latrines. The towers' circular basements, possibly for storage or incarceration, are each lit only by a slit that runs up through the wall. The north-west and south-west towers have four five-sided floors, the middle two chambers each having a fireplace.

The west range contains the kitchen and the great hall, and between them is the buttery and pantry. At one end of the hall there is a passage that connects the inner ward with the outer. A chapel and a bakehouse lie on the north side, together with the well, and there is a doorway here leading to the outer ward and a small twin-towered gatehouse leading to the Castle Rock. On the south side is a granary, and between it and the kitchen is the site of the Ystumgwern Hall, a building that may have been a timber-framed house that was dismantled and re-erected in the castle.

Standing in the outer ward by the hall range, the observant can see from the window openings that the outer skin of masonry on this side was added to the early 1280s walling a few years later, at the same time as the two western corner towers were built. Below the outer ward at this point is the 'way from the sea', a steep passage, which had two gates, that was the point of arrival for anyone coming by sea. Overlooking the 'way' are two rock platforms on which stone-throwing artillery may have been mounted. One other feature of note in the outer ward is the projecting latrine turret in the middle of the southern outer curtain wall.

Tomen y Mur, Merioneth

Ordnance Survey: Landranger 124. *SH: 707 288.*
Access via a footpath.

Just off the A470, north of Trawsfynydd, is a large motte, with a mutilated summit. It is set within a Roman fort, just one of a number of Roman remains in the immediate area, including an amphitheatre. The fort was probably used as the bailey. The castle may owe its origin to the military campaigns of King William II (1087–1100) or King Henry I (1100–35).

1 The motte-and-bailey castle at Sycharth

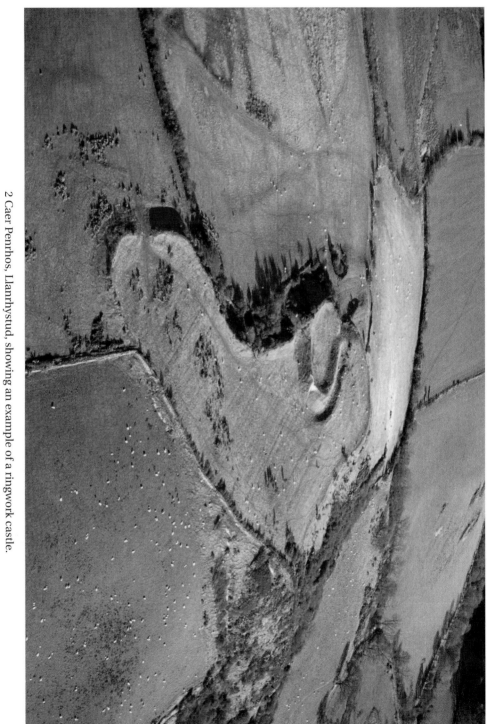

2 Caer Penrhos, Llanrhystud, showing an example of a ringwork castle. Here it has been built within an earlier, prehistoric, hillfort

3 The interior of the chapel at Beaumaris Castle

4 The interior of Conwy Castle, looking west to the town and its walls beyond

5 The gatehouse at Cricieth Castle

6 Harlech Castle viewed from the south

7 Aerial view of Denbigh Castle and town walls

8 Powis Castle from the air

9 Carew Castle, with the Elizabethan long gallery in the centre

10 Dinefwr Castle, with its keep (right) and Edwardian chamber block (left)

11 Kidwelly Castle from the east, with the chapel tower in the centre

12 The round keep of Bronllys Castle

13 The motte and shell keep of Cardiff Castle

14 The fragmentary remains of Castell Dinas

15 An aerial view of Chepstow Castle, overlooking the river Wye

16 The keep and gatehouse at Raglan Castle

3

The North-East

(Denbighshire and Flintshire)

Caergwrle or Hope Castle, Flintshire

Ordnance Survey: Landranger 117. *SJ: 307 572.* Local authority.

Although this hilltop stronghold was the last castle to have been built by a Welsh prince, Dafydd ap Gruffudd, the brother of Llywelyn ap Gruffudd, it was erected with the permission of King Edward in 1277–82, after the first Welsh war. It was from this probably unfinished castle that Dafydd launched his attack on Hawarden Castle in 1282, an event that sparked the second war. Although the Welsh themselves

Owain Glyndŵr's revolt

This rebellion, which was fuelled by growing tension between the Welsh gentry and English officialdom, broke out in 1400, but had all but exhausted itself by about 1410. Its leading figure, Owain Glyndŵr, was himself of princely blood, and during his revolt assumed the title prince of Wales.

The rebellion involved attacks and sieges on a number of castles throughout Wales. The Welsh took three of the Edwardian castles: Aberystwyth and Harlech were held for a number of years, from 1404 until late 1408 or early 1409, whilst Conwy, taken by ruse in early 1401, was back in English control within a few months. Harlech became Owain's headquarters, and the castle's recapture by the future King Henry V is one of the earliest instances of the use of cannon in siege warfare in Wales. However, not every castle siege was successful: Caernarfon Castle and town, with only a small garrison, held out against a combined force of French, Bretons and Welsh, and in south Wales the town of Kidwelly was sacked, but the castle, although damaged, proved too strong for the Welsh.

damaged the castle to prevent its use by the English, it was soon repaired and came into the ownership of King Edward's queen, Eleanor, in 1283, and was known as Hope. Suffering an accidental fire in 1283, probably destroying the newly erected timber buildings, by the early 1300s Caergwrle had become redundant and was in ruins.

At one end of the summit of the hill is a stub of walling, all that is left of a great round tower that the English demolished in 1282. The castle had two other towers, both D-shaped, and parts of the curtain wall survive, one section having latrine chutes. A bank and ditch defend the curtain on this side. Excavations in the interior revealed a bread oven and the well.

The castle sits within a much larger enclosure that is post-Roman in date.

Castell Dinas Brân, Denbighshire

Ordnance Survey: Landranger 117. *SJ: 223 431.*
Guidebook. Local authority.

Set on a hill overlooking the town of Llangollen, and accessible only by steep climbs, this very ruined castle of the Welsh lords of north Powys was built within an Iron Age hillfort in about 1260 (figure 1). It had a short life, as the Welsh abandoned and set fire to it in the war of 1277. Nevertheless, the commander of the advancing English forces, the earl of Lincoln, recommended that it should be garrisoned as it was such a strong fortress. It was in the possession of the earl of Surrey in the 1280s, but it was soon totally abandoned when that earl built the new castle of Holt (p. 48).

Rectangular in plan, and similar to Dolforwyn (p. 54), with rock-cut ditches on three sides, the castle has a rectangular keep at the east end, a small twin-towered gatehouse set below it on the north and the very fragmentary remains of an apsidal tower in the middle of the south curtain, with the site of the hall on its east side. Both the keep and gatehouse had latrines, as shown by the outfall chutes on the south and north sides respectively. The keep probably had just one floor over a basement, the entrance being via a staircase on the west side that led up to the first floor. Few other features survive, but the well was set in the south-east corner of the ditch.

Built of mudstone quarried from the ditches, fragments of carved sandstone masonry indicate that there was more to this castle in terms of quality than the ruins suggest, and that it was once a handsome building.

Chirk Castle, Denbighshire

Ordnance Survey: Landranger 126. *SJ: 268 381.*
Entry charge. Guidebook. National Trust.

Chirk was one a number of so-called lordship castles built by leading lords of King Edward I in the wake of the second Welsh war (1282–3); the others were Denbigh, Hawarden, Holt and Ruthin. The history of Chirk after the Middle Ages, particularly following its destruction in 1659, at the end of the civil war period, has seen this castle transformed into a great country house rather than a castle, but enough remains of the late thirteenth-/early fourteenth-century castle of Roger Mortimer to show that its original form was not unlike the inner ward to be seen at Beaumaris on Anglesey (p. 11), although even less of Chirk was completed to plan. Mortimer was given estates here by King Edward I following the second Welsh campaign, and the castle has been occupied virtually ever since, becoming the home of the Myddleton family from the late sixteenth century.

Three medieval great towers remain, although one, the Middle Tower, has been 'hollowed out' to take the grand staircase of 1777–8, and at some stage the upper storey in each tower was removed, assuming of course that these floors were built. The entrance today is simply a passage between the Middle Tower and the later seventeenth-century Bachelor's Tower, and if the castle originally had a great gatehouse elsewhere, no trace survives. The Old Maid's Tower is also of the seventeenth century, as is the east range, from which the tower projects, with its fine long gallery.

The south range, incorporating the chapel, dates to the fifteenth century, whilst the north range, built against the medieval curtain wall, belongs to the time of the first Myddeltons, about 1600. The nineteenth and early twentieth centuries saw further alteration and restoration.

A feel for the medieval castle as originally built is best obtained from Adam's Tower on the west side and the adjacent curtain wall, although the tower's windows were altered subsequently. Two shafts light the basement, perhaps a prison, as may have been the room above, in the manner of the Prison Tower at Conwy. Just off the Muniment Room, on the first floor of the tower, is a room in which three murder holes are set in the floor.

Denbigh Castle and town walls, Denbighshire

Ordnance Survey: Landranger 116. *SJ: 052 658.*
Entry charge. Guidebook. Cadw.

Like Chirk, Denbigh was a lordship castle (plate 7; figure 6). Denbigh was built on or near the site of a residence of the Welsh princes, known as a *llys*, during the second Welsh war, after King Edward I granted the district to one of his leading commanders, Henry de Lacy, earl of Lincoln. In October 1282 the earl and his king met to discuss the construction of the new castle.

The initial phase, from the end of 1282, saw the construction of a large walled circuit with some D-shaped or half-round towers and gatehouses that formed both the outer wall of the castle and the town defences. That section of the castle that largely sits within the medieval town is very different in style to the initial phase, for here we have massive polygonal towers, including a triple-towered gatehouse that even in its ruined state is a wonder of medieval construction. The exterior of the towers is remarkable for the chequerboard decoration of different coloured sandstones.

Like Caernarfon, Denbigh fell to the Welsh in the uprising of 1294, led in the north by Madog ap Llywelyn (see p. 55), and this may have been because, again like Caernarfon, the frontage of the castle that faced into the town had not been completed to any great height. So, when the castle was recaptured at the end of 1294, work resumed on the northern and eastern defences, although we cannot be sure that the castle, especially the gatehouse, had ever been completed to plan by the time of Earl Henry's death in 1311.

Although the town below the castle was damaged during the early 1400s, during the Glyndŵr revolt, the castle appears to have held out. It again saw military service in the civil wars of the 1640s, when it was held by the royalists. Besieged for several months in 1646, it fell to the parliamentarian army in late October. Unlike many castles, it was not dismantled (slighted) following its capture, as the castle was used to imprison royalists. However, much of the curtain wall and two towers was deliberately destroyed following the restoration of the monarchy in 1660.

The entrance to the castle, above the broad arch of which is the statue of a king, possibly Edward II (1307–27), was originally reached via a drawbridge. Then one proceeded through a passage heavily

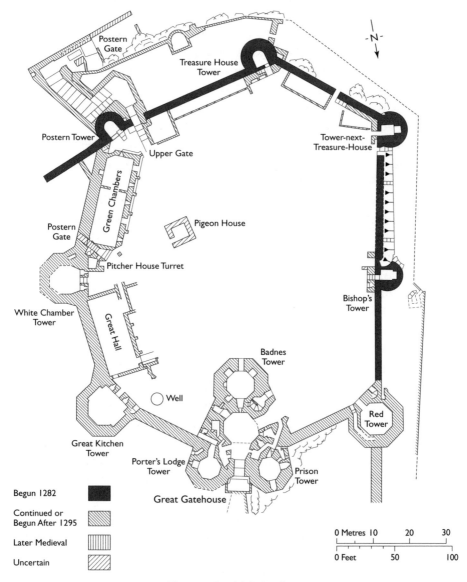

Figure 6: Denbigh Castle

defended by murder holes, doorways and two portcullises before reaching an octagonal vaulted hall framed by the three towers. In order to reach the courtyard one had to pass through another door with a portcullis. Although the upper floors of the three towers and the area over the entrance hall provided a number of private rooms, one of the two outer towers of the gatehouse was named the Prison Tower, since its ground-floor chamber and the basement below were used for the incarceration of felons.

The eastern side of the castle has two great polygonal towers, the Great Kitchen and the White Chamber towers, and running along the inner face of the curtain wall here lay the chapel, the great hall and a block of apartments called the Green Chambers. Between the latter and the White Chamber Tower was a small doorway or postern leading out to the town walls. The existence of the site of a sink, together with various drains, suggests that the basement of the Green Chambers was used to store wine and meat, while above would have been a fine suite of chambers for accommodation.

Past the Green Chambers is one of the towers of the first phase, and this was incorporated into a more sophisticated upper gate with a staggered and well-defended approach after 1294. The 1280s curtain wall continues round to the main front of the castle via three small towers, meeting the large polygonal Red Tower. Following the castle's recapture from the Welsh in 1294, a thin outer wall known as a mantlet was built as part of the upper gate's new defences; another mantlet paralleled the curtain wall running south from the Red Tower. A feature of interest in this latter section is the postern or sallyport provided with its own small portcullis, as well as murder holes.

The town wall runs from the Red Tower, soon meeting the Exchequer Gate, the foundations of which are visible. It appears to have been similar to the Burgess Gate, rectangular in plan at ground-floor level, but round fronted on the upper floors. The town wall continues without towers, and largely hidden by houses, to the Burgess Gate, the upper part of which shows the same marvellous chequerboard stonework seen at the castle. The gate originally had a drawbridge, a portcullis, a doorway, murder holes and arrowslits. The two rooms above – one with a latrine, the other with a fireplace – were linked to the town wall on either side.

The eastern section of the town wall is the best preserved. A locked gate (key from the castle) gives access to the wall, which leads to a tower at the north-eastern corner, and on to the Countess Tower. From here, the 1280s wall runs back up to the castle, the only mural tower being the Bastion Tower not far from the castle. However, the defences were enlarged to the south of the Countess Tower after 1294 to create a salient that incorporated an important supply of water, augmenting the well in the castle. The focal point of this stretch is the Goblin Tower in which the well is situated. It was against this section of the town's defences that Parliament's artillery was directed in 1646 in order to deprive the royalists of water.

Ewloe Castle, Flintshire

Ordnance Survey: Landranger 117. *SJ: 288 675.*
Guidebook. Cadw.

If any monument represents Llywelyn ap Gruffudd's growing power in Wales it is Ewloe Castle (figure 1), positioned as it was (and is) right on the border with England, only a few miles from the great city and stronghold of Chester. This area of north-east Wales was regained by Llywelyn in 1257, and, although various arguments have been put forward for the dating of the castle, it is now generally accepted that it was built soon after 1257, with the inner ward constructed before the outer.

Llywelyn built the castle within the medieval forest of Ewloe and in 1265 he went on from his position of power to destroy the neighbouring English castle of Hawarden, later to be rebuilt in the 1280s (very occasionally open to the public). However, as a result of the first Welsh war of 1277 Llywelyn lost most of his territorial possessions outside north-west Wales and Ewloe virtually disappears from history. A document of 1311, the only record that mentions the castle, states that it was 'in great part standing'.

Defended by a ditch on two sides, the core of the castle is the stone enclosure of the inner or upper ward. In it sits the main tower, an elongated apsidal structure of a type to be seen at other native Welsh castles, such as Castell y Bere (p. 19). The original entrance to the upper ward was over a bridge and through a simple doorway on the north-east side. A staircase, with a doorway at the foot, led up to the first-floor entrance of the tower, and from there a mural stairway led on up to the battlements. The basement would have been accessible only through a trapdoor in the floor of the main room, and presumably was used for storage. The hall or chamber on the first floor has two windows, and there may have been a third in the now collapsed north wall of the tower.

Both ends of the curtain wall of the outer or lower ward butt up against the upper ward, rather than being bonded with it, and this suggests that it was added later, but probably soon after the initial phase. The enclosure, dominated by the circular west tower, would originally have been full of wooden buildings, but nothing survives today.

Flint Castle, Flintshire

Ordnance Survey: Landranger 117. *SJ: 247 733.*
Guidebook. Cadw.

This castle (figure 7) was the product of King Edward I's first Welsh war of 1277, built a day's march from Chester. Work began on it and the adjacent new town on a fresh site in the summer of 1277, making it the first of the king's castles in north Wales. By 1284 most of the castle had been built, at a cost of about £7,000, but the building accounts suggest that there was not one continuous building programme, and that the castle may have been damaged in the war of 1282–3.

The town was certainly damaged in 1282, during the second Welsh war, and again in the revolt of 1294–5 when the constable of the castle set fire to it to prevent the Welsh from using it. In the civil wars of the 1640s, both sides held the castle at various times, and, although it was garrisoned by Parliament after its capture in 1646, the castle was made unusable the following year.

The castle, originally set within a moat fed by the sea, has a large outer bailey, with some of the curtain wall surviving, and the remains of the outer gate has been excavated archaeologically. There are circular mural towers at three corners of the square inner ward; their upper floors provided accommodation. Arrowslits can be seen in the towers and also those parts of the curtain wall that still survive to a reasonable height. The traces of internal buildings evident in the inner ward date to more recent times; the original medieval buildings are likely to have been of timber, and built against curtain walls.

The most remarkable feature of Flint is the great circular keep, even in its truncated state. It stands detached from the main body of the castle, possibly in its own moat. There is nothing comparable to it in western Europe, let alone Britain. A bridge with a drawbridge would have provided access to the doorway (no portcullis), and steps lead down to a mural gallery with arrowslits, and a well. A hole in the roof over the well shows that water could be brought up by bucket to the floor above. Vertical chutes in the walls were for the latrines on the upper floor(s), which emptied into the moat, to be cleansed by the tide.

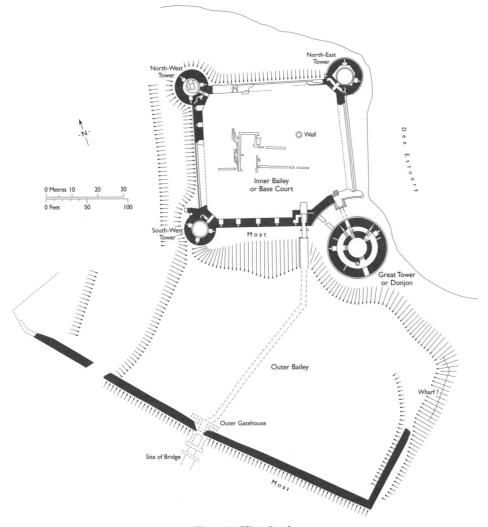

Figure 7: Flint Castle

A circular basement sits in the centre of the keep, now open to the elements. The first floor is the only upper level that survives, but there must have been at least a second storey. On this floor five chambers run off from the centre of the tower, one of which was a chapel. When in 1301 the castle passed into the hands of Edward, prince of Wales, the future King Edward II, a new timber structure was added to the top of the keep.

The town was only ever defended by an earthen rampart and timber palisade; the streets of the town today still reflect the grid pattern as laid down in 1277.

Holt Castle, Denbighshire

Ordnance Survey: Landranger 117. *SJ: 412 537.* **Open access.**

This was one of King Edward I's 'lordship' castles, built by John de Warenne, earl of Surrey, soon after 1282, but it may not have been completed until the early 1300s, by Warenne's grandson. It saw action

Gatehouses

Motte and ringwork castles would have had timber gatehouses or gateways, but only a few have been excavated. Excavations at Rumney Castle (Cae Castell) near Cardiff and Penmaen Castle, Gower, both in Glamorgan, revealed posthole evidence for the timber entrance. The original structure at both these castles is likely to have been a wooden battlemented platform or roofed chamber over the entrance passage. Such simple structures, but translated into masonry, can be seen at castles such as Ogmore (p. 129), whilst other Norman stone castles often had a simple gateway built adjacent to a mural tower or keep, as at Newcastle in Bridgend (p. 97).

From the late twelfth century twin-towered gatehouses are added to castles, reaching a peak in sophistication in the late thirteenth century at castles such as Beaumaris and Harlech. The entrance passages were heavily defended, often with some combination of drawbridges, double-leaf doors, arrowslits, portcullises, murder holes, machicolations and guard chambers. The upper floors often provided accommodation for the constable of the castle or important guests, and could include a chapel and sometimes even a small kitchen.

in the civil war of the 1640s, but was then systematically robbed for its building stone for Eaton Hall in 1675–83.

A footpath leads down to the boss of rock by the river Dee that supports the fragments of this once great castle. The curtain that survives represents the inner face of the inner walls that framed the courtyard, with a doorway evident. Gone are the five circular mural towers and entrance that we know from the plan and elevation of 1562 that is held by the British Library in London. There was also a square tower that was the water gate.

Rhuddlan Castle, Flintshire

Ordnance Survey: Landranger 116. *SJ: 024 779.*
Entry charge. Guidebook. Cadw.

The first castle at Rhuddlan was the motte and bailey know as Twthill a few hundred metres south-east of the stone castle, although there was a Welsh palace here long before. The motte, accessible to the public, was built by Robert of Rhuddlan in 1073, and survived as an earth-and-timber castle well into the thirteenth century, changing hands several times between the Normans/English and the Welsh.

All this was to change as a result of King Edward I's war of 1277, for a new castle (figure 8) was begun here in the summer of that year, soon after Flint had been started, and work continued until early 1282, costing almost £10,000. Further work on accommodation was paid for from 1283 until 1286, work that included a chapel for the use of Queen Eleanor. Adjacent to the castle was a new town with earth-and-timber defences; a section of the earth bank still survives.

Like Flint, the town was damaged in the Glyndŵr uprising in 1400, although the castle held out. Like many other Welsh castles, it was held for the king in the civil war of the 1640s, but was taken in 1646 and partly demolished two years later.

If anything emphasizes the importance of sea, as well as land, routes in the positioning of the Edwardian castles in north Wales, Rhuddlan is a case in point. The river Clwyd that flows past the castle had to be canalized so that shipping could access the castle and its defensible dock, set below the main body of the castle, work that initially involved many hundreds of diggers from diverse parts of England.

The castle had seven entrances, ranging from gatehouses to small posterns: four into the outer ward and three into the inner ward. Of the outer gateways, one lay against Gillot's Tower which commanded the dock, and there was a small entrance or postern in the river wall; there are a number of arrowslits visible where this wall survives to some

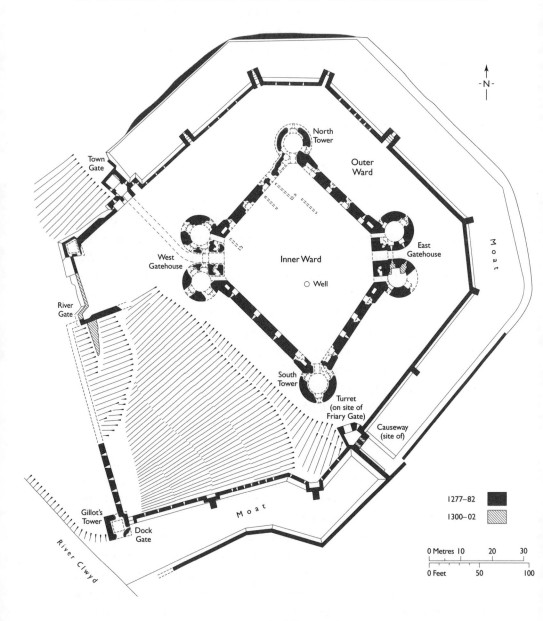

Figure 8: Rhuddlan Castle

height. Friary Gate on the eastern side was soon to be blocked up and converted into a turret (1300–2). The main entrance to the outer ward was that from the new borough, the Town Gate. Although much of the curtain wall of the outer ward has been robbed, enough remains to show how it revetted the dry moat on three sides of the castle, and that it had a number of turrets with steps (some later being blocked) that enabled defenders to access the moat from under cover. The wall also displays the remains of a large number of arrowslits that enabled archers to fire down into the moat, whilst other archers could also use loops set higher in the curtain to fire beyond the moat.

The castle's big defended entrances, each originally with a gate and portcullis, were the west and east twin-towered gatehouses in two corners of the diamond-shaped inner ward; stone robbing has, however, removed evidence for many of the original features of the west gatehouse. The other two corners each have a circular tower, a small postern gate being adjacent to the north tower. Five of the six inner ward towers had four floors each for accommodation, but the south tower has five. The towers are all linked by a curtain wall that survives up to the wall-walks, even though the crenellated battlements no longer exist. Two features to note in the curtains are the thickening against the towers, to accommodate latrine chutes, and the remains of small projections in the centres of the curtains that are all that are left of what are known as box machicolations, which permitted defenders to drop missiles on attackers below.

Although the inner ward looks bare today, it would originally have been full of timber buildings, providing additional accommodation as well as services, including halls either side of a central kitchen.

Sycharth, Denbighshire

Ordnance Survey: Landranger 126. *SJ: 204 258*.
Permission to be sought from owner.

This is a fine motte-and-bailey castle (plate 1). It is not known when it was built, but its classic form suggest a twelfth-century date, unless it was built in an archaic form in the fourteenth century. Its claim to fame is as the home of Owain Glyndŵr, when it had a handsome timber-framed building on the motte. The whole complex is described in flowery fashion by the poet Iolo Goch in a poem of about 1390. It was destroyed by the English in 1403 during the Glyndŵr revolt.

Beside the motte and bailey, there are also fishponds below the castle which may have formed part of the manorial complex.

Tomen y Rhodwydd, Denbighshire

Ordnance Survey: Landranger 116. *SJ: 177 516.*
Permission to be sought from owner.

Although on private land, but visible from the road, this castle is included because it is one of the finest motte-and-bailey castles in Wales. Originally built by Owain Gwynedd, lord of north Wales, in 1149, it was strengthened, with its ditches re-dug, by the English in 1212 at the time of King John's second campaign in north Wales.

4

Central

(Cardiganshire, Montgomeryshire and Radnorshire)

Aberystwyth Castle, Cardiganshire

Ordnance Survey: Landranger 135. *SN: 579 815.*
Guidebook. Local authority.

In the summer of 1277, while King Edward I waged his first Welsh war and the construction began on his newly founded castles in north Wales, Flint and Rhuddlan, work also started on the new royal castle of Aberystwyth. The seafront castle cost just over £4,000 and, although construction ran on to 1289, the majority of the expenditure occurred in the first three years. In 1280–1 very little work was undertaken, and the lack of preparedness of the castle was the subject of a scathing report by a royal official. It was no wonder that after the outbreak of the second Welsh war in 1282 the castle and its walled town were taken and burnt by the Welsh. In the revolt of 1294 the castle held out since it could be supplied by sea, but this did not help it in the early 1400s when it was eventually taken by Owain Glyndŵr. In 1406 Owain repulsed one English siege by Prince Henry, the future King Henry V, but in a second siege two years later Henry recovered the castle. On the eve of the English civil war (1642–6) a royal mint was established in the castle. Aberystwyth was held for the king in the wars, but taken by Parliament in 1646 and much of it was blown up. What survived was used over the ensuing years as a source of building stone for the town, and as a result the castle is a poor shadow of its former self.

The castle is lozenge or diamond shaped, and in its final form was fully concentric in plan, with an inner ward enveloped by a narrow outer ward. Another enclosure to the north has been lost to the sea. Archaeological excavations, however, have shown that originally the castle was not fully concentric, for there was no inner west curtain;

this was to be built after the 1282–3 war as part of the repairs undertaken.

In the east angle of the curtain a small twin-towered gatehouse gave access to the outer ward and to the great inner gatehouse, and at the other three angles of both wards there were originally round or D-shaped towers, with another tower midway along the inner curtain on the south-western side. The tallest surviving part of the castle is a semicircular tower on the north-western side of the inner ward. A postern gate in its base led to a small twin-towered gate to the now vanished third enclosure.

The great gatehouse had stair turrets to the rear, and between it and the southern tower was the hall.

Dolforwyn Castle, Montgomeryshire

Ordnance Survey: Landranger 136. *SO: 152 950.*
Guidebook. Cadw.

This is one of the most significant castles in Wales (figure 1), for it was the last one to have been built by an independent prince of Wales, Llywelyn ap Gruffudd. Caergwrle (p. 39) was constructed a few years later by Llywelyn's brother, Dafydd, but that work was undertaken under the auspices of the English Crown.

Dolforwyn, a hilltop castle with rock-cut ditches, was under construction from 1273. Located on a ridge in a politically sensitive area, it was within Llywelyn's territory, as agreed in 1267 in the Treaty of Montgomery, but nevertheless close to the English March and the royal castle and town of Montgomery a few miles away to the north-east. In the war of 1277 Dolforwyn was the target of an English army's drive from Montgomery. In spite of the bombardment of the English siege engines, it would appear that it was the lack of water, coupled with Llywelyn's failure to lift the siege, which forced the garrison to surrender on 8 April 1277 to Roger Mortimer (d.1282). The recent excavations found the remains of some of the stone shot that had been fired by the siege engines.

The castle was granted to Roger Mortimer the following year. Following its capture and into the fourteenth century, Roger and successive Mortimer lords undertook much rebuilding at Dolforwyn. However, by 1398 it was recorded as being ruinous, and such was its state of collapse over the centuries that only a stub of masonry was visible in the twentieth century, before the excavations of 1982 to 2002. The excavations, however, have uncovered the whole castle, so that it is open to public view, following its consolidation and interpretation.

The Welsh phase of this rectangular castle can be divided into two, with the keep and the round tower at the west and east ends of the castle respectively being built first, but soon followed by the curtain walls which butt against these towers, and the D-shaped tower midway along the north curtain wall. The courtyard was divided into two by a rock-cut ditch, spanned by a bridge, but this was filled in after the siege. Although there were some internal buildings, it would seem that most of these structures had not been built by the time of the siege. The majority of the courtyard buildings that were excavated date to the English period, including the well, the lack of which had helped to prompt the Welsh surrender in 1277.

The main entrance was at the west end of the ridge, through a simple gateway reached by a bridge, but overlooked by the rectangular keep, and, after the siege, by a guardroom. A smaller gateway lay in the middle of the south curtain, but this was to be blocked by the Mortimers. The keep originally consisted of an upper floor over a basement, a flight of steps leading up to its entrance. Some time after the siege a doorway was inserted at ground level into the basement, this area then being divided into two unequal chambers. The larger of

ɱadog ap Llywelyn's revolt

Madog ap Llywelyn, a cousin of Llywelyn ap Gruffudd, but who may have served with the English in the war of 1277, rose up in rebellion in September 1294 in the north-west, and the ultimately short-lived uprising spread throughout most of Wales. Disputes with English officialdom in the north-west counties and the harsh tax assessment of 1292–3 were the sparks that ignited the flame.

A number of castles were besieged, and some even taken, notably Caernarfon, where considerable damage ensued (see p. 15). Madog, who styled himself prince of Wales, was defeated at the battle of Maes Moydog, near Welshpool, in March 1295; he himself escaped, but was captured that summer, and was still a prisoner in 1312. It is not known when he died.

the two had the floor above removed so that it was open to the keep's roof, providing a fine chamber, lit by a new window that overlooked the courtyard. Other work on the keep after the siege included the rebuilding of one corner damaged in the 1277 attack.

In the north-east corner of the courtyard, running east from the north tower, was a two-storey building that was the only domestic range that Llywelyn had time to construct before the siege. The upper floor may have been designed as the prince's personal hall or chamber; it had a hearth in the floor supported by a pillar in the room below, the remains of which can still be seen. West of the north tower was a hall of the post-siege period, and by the tower is the well added to the castle after 1277. On the other side of the courtyard were service rooms added by the Mortimers, a bake- and brewhouse standing close to the keep, with a long timber-framed storeroom running from this range up to the round tower. Three ovens are visible in the bakehouse, whilst the discovery of brewing vats and other features in the recent excavations showed that the adjacent room was the brewhouse.

The round tower stands at the east end of the castle, overlooking the rock-cut ditch and the ridge beyond. Unusually, there appears to have been a doorway at ground-floor level from the beginning, but the main floor lay above on the first floor, the doorway to which was reached by an external staircase. Traces of the mortar rendering that originally covered the tower, and other parts of the castle, to make it weatherproof still survive. This protective coating was needed because much of the local stone from which Dolforwyn was built was of a friable and poor quality.

A number of chutes can be seen in the external walls, indicating the provision of latrines in various areas of the castle.

Montgomery Castle, Montgomeryshire

Ordnance Survey: Landranger 137. *SO: 221 967.*
Guidebook. Cadw.

The campaign into mid Wales in 1223, while King Henry III (1216–72) was still a minor, was to result in the construction of this castle that stands on a hill overlooking the town of Montgomery. The castle was the successor to a motte and bailey a short distance away to the north known as Hen Domen (Old Mound). This earth-and-timber castle, lying close to the river Severn and the strategic river crossing of Rhyd Chwima, has been one of the most systematically excavated castles in Britain. It was built by Roger of Montgomery, earl of Shrewsbury, soon after the Norman Conquest, and it remained in use even into the thirteenth century, when it acted as an outpost to the new castle. Hen Domen is on private land and permission to visit must be sought from the adjacent farm.

The instigator of the new castle at Montgomery was the king's right-hand man, the justiciar Hubert de Burgh (d.1243). He was a man who had experienced castle warfare at first hand, latterly in the successful defence of Dover Castle against the French in 1216, and was also involved in castle building, such as at his castles of Grosmont and Skenfrith in Monmouthshire (pp. 142, 143). In spite of being overlooked by the old Iron Age hillfort of Ffridd Faldwyn a little distance away to the west, the new castle has commanding views of the surrounding countryside. At the foot of the hill a new town was founded at the same time.

The initial work at the castle involved cutting through the rock to form ditches and erecting temporary prefabricated timber defences.

Mural towers

Although the Normans would have been familiar with Roman fortifications in Britain and on the Continent, many with projecting towers or bastions (for example, see Caerwent's Roman defences), we do not find examples of mural towers in masonry castles until the late twelfth century. Dover in Kent has some of the earliest examples. They become more common from the early thirteenth century, and numerous examples can be seen in Wales.

A mural tower could serve one or more functions. It was designed as a platform for the defenders of a castle or town wall; it provided accommodation, for a number were equipped with fireplaces and latrines; it could be used for storage, such use usually assigned to the basement; and one or more floors could be used as a prison. A tower might also house a chapel.

There is evidence that some earth-and-timber motte and baileys had wooden mural towers. The painstakingly thorough excavations of the northern half of the bailey at Hen Domen, Montgomeryshire – the first Montgomery Castle – found evidence for such towers. However, it is only through excavation that such evidence can be found, and even then it may be open to alternative explanations.

In 1224, work on the masonry defences of the inner ward began, but the middle ward's timber palisade remained until the 1250s. By 1228, over £3,600 had been spent on the castle, cost that included payment of the garrison, as well as deforesting the terrain to the west to ensure that the Welsh could not get close enough to surprise the castle. In 1233, a tower, perhaps the gatehouse, was roofed in lead, whilst a year later the well tower had to be repaired. Structural problems with the well tower led to its almost complete rebuilding in the fourteenth century.

In the 1250s, the middle ward's defences were rebuilt in stone, with a twin-towered outer gatehouse. A new range was built around this ward in the 1530s by Bishop Rowland Lee, lord president of the Council of Wales and the Marches, and almost a century later, in the 1620s, Edward Herbert built a fine brick house in the same area. It is our loss that this fine building was razed to the ground in 1649, after the civil war, and the medieval castle was similarly slighted.

The middle ward is reached by passing a series of outworks that guarded the medieval approach, including a D-shaped mound that was enclosed or revetted by a stone wall. Passing over the bridge to the footings of the outer gate and into the middle ward, there is below to the right a circular structure, a dovecote associated with the Herbert house. Archaeological excavation has shown that the parliamentarian garrison cast musket and pistol shot here during the civil war. The middle ward contains the footings of the sixteenth- and seventeenth-century houses, as well as a medieval kiln house for drying grain built against the eastern curtain wall. There are a number of solid medieval turrets projecting from the eastern curtain and these may have had wooden platforms on them for defence.

A modern bridge crosses the wide and deep rock-cut inner ditch, leading to the remains of the inner ward's twin-towered gatehouse. The ditch is protected at each end by a wall with a small doorway or postern set into it. In the gatehouse passage, which was originally protected by two pairs of doors and a portcullis, a doorway opens into a chamber in the west tower, but this doorway was a later medieval addition, for originally access to this room was via a trapdoor in the floor above. The entrance to the larger ground-floor room in the east gatehouse tower, the guardroom or porter's lodge, was from within the inner ward itself. An external wooden staircase at the back of the gatehouse led up to the upper floors. Projecting from the rear of the gatehouse there was a timber-framed chapel at first-floor level.

The inner ward would have contained the principal accommodation of the castle in the Middle Ages. Beyond the gatehouse is the well tower, where in 1223 miners from the Forest of Dean in Gloucestershire started to excavate the well shaft to a depth of about 210 feet (64 metres). In 1973–4 archaeological excavations found a range of material in the shaft, including a medieval bucket and a civil war leather pistol holster. Built against the north wall of the well tower was the kitchen, with a brewhouse beyond, and projecting from the north end of the inner ward there are the remains of a semicircular tower.

New Radnor, Radnorshire

Ordnance Survey: Landranger 148. *SO: 212 608.* Local trust.

The massive earthworks, owned by a trust but freely accessible, are all that remain of this thirteenth-century castle, the successor to Old Radnor. The rough summit of the castle mound may indicate masonry, and below it is the bailey with deep ditches. The tree-lined bank represents the defences of the associated medieval town, which was laid out on a grid pattern. The town ramparts would have supported a palisade rather than a stone wall, permission being given for the construction in 1257 when Roger Mortimer received what is known as a murage grant from the Crown.

New Radnor town may have been taken, or at least attacked, by Owain Glyndŵr in 1401, although the castle was reported to be in a state of readiness in 1405. The castle and town defences are likely to have been left to deteriorate during the fifteenth century.

Painscastle, Radnorshire

Ordnance Survey: Landranger 148. *SO: 167 461.*
Permission to be sought from owner.

This is a magnificent motte-and-bailey castle, and well worth obtaining the necessary permission from the adjacent farm to view it. Like New Radnor, the grass may well conceal the foundations of stone walls.

The castle may have been established in the first half of the twelfth century, but the Welsh chronicles record that King Henry III built, that is to say rebuilt, it in 1231, and the masonry may belong to this period.

It was destroyed by Llywelyn ap Gruffudd in 1265, but occupied briefly in 1405 when the castle, amongst others, was ordered to be manned as a defence against the Welsh under Glyndŵr.

Powis Castle, Montgomeryshire

Ordnance Survey: Landranger 126. *SO: 268 381*.
Entry charge. Guidebook. National Trust.

Like Chirk (p. 41), this castle is medieval in origin, but has been almost continuously occupied since the Middle Ages (plate 8). The accretion of later buildings and much modification have made it notoriously difficult to interpret the early phasing, even harder than it is at Chirk.

The earliest masonry is the curving wall on the south side of the main structure that encompasses a minute courtyard, the inner ward. It appears to date to the middle of the thirteenth century, and was probably built by the Welsh lord of Powys, Gruffudd ap Gwenwynwyn. Llywelyn ap Gruffudd destroyed Gruffudd's castle in 1274, but, following the English victory in the first Welsh war, Gruffudd was able to regain his lands and rebuild his castle. This second phase may include the east gate, then the main entrance, and the adjacent keep-like tower in the south-eastern corner of the inner ward.

In the fourteenth century Powis came into the hands of John Charlton through marriage. Charlton became an important royal official in the reigns of Edward II (1307–27) and Edward III (1327–77) and it would seem that he transformed the castle. A new gatehouse, with portcullises, was built, facing into Wales. This twin-towered structure became the main entrance, reached by passing through the outer ward, the north wall of which, with its D-shaped tower, is medieval.

Powis came into the hands of the Herbert family in the sixteenth century, later to become earls of Powis, and the current earl still resides in the castle. Garrisoned in the civil war in the 1640s, the castle underwent a major rebuild in the later seventeenth century, with a new state bedroom and a magnificent grand staircase. Further improvements were made in the late eighteenth century and again in 1815–18, as well as in the early twentieth century. These later phases, and the association of Powis with Robert Clive (Clive of India), are well told in the National Trust guidebook.

Presteigne (The Warden), Radnorshire

This castle stands on a ridge just outside Presteigne and has open access, having been presented to the town in 1805, at a time when it was a pleasure garden.

The castle is a ringwork and bailey, first mentioned in the first half of the thirteenth century, but probably founded by the Mortimer family in the second half of the previous century. It was destroyed by Llywelyn ap Gruffudd in 1262.

Grassy mounds indicate the presence of stone defences, and there may have been a gatehouse to both the bailey and the ringwork.

Tinboeth, Radnorshire

The climb to this hilltop site is rewarded by superb views of the surrounding country, access to the remains of this castle being permitted by the owner.

The fragment of surviving masonry from a gatehouse or tower has recently been conserved, but the rest of the castle today is earthwork and buried or fallen masonry. In origin, the castle would appear to have been a ringwork, possibly within an Iron Age hillfort. Its early history is obscure, but it may have been built by the Braose family in the twelfth century before passing into the hands of the Mortimers in the middle of the next century. Work on the castle may have been undertaken around 1316, but the castle was certainly ruinous by the sixteenth century.

5

The South-West
(Carmarthenshire and Pembrokeshire)

Carew Castle, Pembrokeshire

Ordnance Survey: Landranger 158. *SN: 047 038.*
Entry charge. Guidebook. National Park.

Carew (plate 9) is famous for three monuments: the eleventh-century cross, the tidal mill and the medieval castle that stands between the two. Although these have been described in some detail by various authors, we must await the results of the excavations and architectural analysis by the University of Wales, Lampeter, for a fuller understanding of the early history of this castle.

The castle sits on a ridge above a tidal estuary, an area that excavations have shown was defended by a series of banks and ditches, probably of Iron Age date, although occupation seems to have lasted into the early Middle Ages. The castle was founded by Gerald of Windsor in about 1100, but we cannot be certain of the form that his castle took. The earliest masonry is the Old Tower, now incorporated into the main fabric of the late thirteenth-/early fourteenth-century castle, but which is likely to have been standing before 1200, either as the detached main tower of what otherwise was still a timber castle or as the castle's gatehouse.

From the late 1200s, the castle was owned by the Carew family; Nicholas (d.1311) and his son John (d.1324) were the men responsible for much of the structure that we see today. The castle was later obtained from the family by Sir Rhys ap Thomas, one of the leading supporters of the Tudor dynasty and King Henry VII (1485–1509), and he undertook some rebuilding, including new windows. Rhys held a great tournament at Carew in 1507 to mark his entry into the ranks of the Knights of the Garter.

Later in the sixteenth century, in 1558, Carew came into the possession of Sir John Perrot, a man who was later to serve as the queen's deputy in Ireland. As well as undertaking work at Laugharne Castle (p. 79), he totally rebuilt the north range of Carew. However, he never finished it, nor the various outbuildings in the outer ward to the east. Viewed from across the water from the northern bank of the estuary, this range, with its long gallery on the uppermost floor, is one of the most remarkable buildings of Elizabethan Wales. Perrot died of natural causes in 1592, after having been committed to the Tower of London on a charge of treason, dying just before he would have been sentenced (or pardoned). The inventory of the castle's contents taken after his death states that there was a locked room that housed a considerable amount of glass that had yet to be placed into various windows, presumably in the north range which was by then already floored and roofed.

Carew continued to be inhabited until the later seventeenth century. In the 1640s, both the royalists and the parliamentarians held the castle at different times, and at that time an angled outwork or redan was built in front of the middle gate to reinforce the approach to the main entrance, as at Manorbier (p. 86) and Newcastle Emlyn (p. 89). The medieval south range of the castle, including the kitchen tower, was demolished during or soon after the wars to make Carew indefensible.

Excavations revealed the footings of the gatehouse to the outer ward, to the south of the walled garden. Beyond is the middle ward with a gatehouse, added by Rhys ap Thomas, projecting from the late thirteenth-century curtain wall. This gate probably provided accommodation for a porter or gatekeeper; an external staircase led to an upper room furnished with a fireplace and a latrine.

Entering the middle ward, walling, possibly of the 1640s, runs across from the chapel tower to the south-east tower and behind it rises the east range consisting of a ground floor, or basement, with two upper storeys. Incorporated into this range is the so-called Old Tower, with a fine Tudor oriel window. By about the year 1200, the tower may have flanked the entrance to the Norman inner ward, whilst to the north and south there was a curtain wall culminating in two towers – the south-east one later formed part of the late thirteenth-century D-shaped tower, whilst part of the north-east or Great Turret became a corner of the chapel tower. Beyond lies one end of the Perrot range, with its fine, partly restored, Elizabethan windows.

The simple gatehouse into the inner ward had murder holes in the passage roof and a portcullis at the inner end. Entering the inner ward, the east side was thickened in the early Tudor period and provided with new windows. Internally, there was a medieval hall on the first floor, over a vaulted undercroft, and this was linked to the first-floor chapel, with an adjacent priest's room and nearby latrine. Above the hall there is a Tudor chamber, the importance of which is signified by the fortunate survival of a beautiful heraldic fireplace.

Turning to the west side of the inner ward, here we have the splendour of the great range of around 1300, enhanced in the early Tudor period by Rhys ap Thomas. His work included a two-storey porch added to the southern end, incorporating the coats of arms of King Henry VII, Prince Arthur (the elder brother of the future Henry VIII) and Katherine of Aragon, and an oriel window at the north end. The great medieval hall, with Tudor improvements, lay on the first floor, and had a fireplace in its eastern and western walls. A massive tower stands at each end of the hall, and, with fireplaces and latrines on the upper floors, and these towers, strengthened with spur buttresses, provided the private accommodation of the Carews.

When Perrot built the north range in the later sixteenth century not only was the original medieval curtain demolished, but the new wing was constructed beyond the original line of the defences, so that the eastern side of the medieval north-west tower became the western end wall of the new range. No great Elizabethan house, even where a medieval castle was being adapted as here and at Raglan (p. 134), was without its long gallery; well heated and hung with panelling, portraits and tapestries, it would have provided an ideal area for social activity.

Carmarthen Castle, Carmarthenshire

**Ordnance Survey: Landranger 159. *SN: 413 200.*
Guidebook. Local authority.**

Until very recently, little was to be seen of this castle, one of the most important in south Wales, and the centre of Anglo-Norman government in this part of the country. Even the gatehouse was tucked away, almost out of sight. The removal of some buildings and campaigns of excavation and conservation have all led to a greater awareness of the remains.

King Henry I (1100–35) established the castle around 1106, on high ground above the river Tywi. The twelfth-century history of Carmarthen is shared with many other castles in the south-west, with numerous Welsh attacks, as well as its capture in 1137. However, during the ascendancy of the Lord Rhys (d.1197) Carmarthen was one of the few castles to remain under Norman control. It was destroyed by the Welsh in 1215, but soon after retaken and rebuilt, remaining in English hands, apart from a short period in 1403, when it was taken by the supporters of Owain Glyndŵr.

Carmarthen was a motte and bailey, and may have remained an earth-and-timber castle until the early thirteenth century, although £170 was spent on it in 1182–3, which may have been for the work that enclosed the motte in a stone wall. After the castle had been retaken in 1223 a considerable amount of work was undertaken to make Carmarthen a strong masonry castle. The motte appears to have had a round tower built on it, and mural towers were added to the inner bailey. There was also a gatehouse, although the present appearance of much of this structure dates to around 1408, when the castle was repaired after its recapture by the Crown. We know from royal documents that there were a number of major domestic buildings within the castle, including as a hall, chapel, kitchen and stable, as one would expect in any stronghold as important as Carmarthen.

It was held for the king in the civil wars of the 1640s, and soon after considerable demolition took place, so that over the ensuing years buildings grew up in and around the castle, obscuring much of what was left. A prison was built on the site, but later demolished to make way for the County Hall (1938–56), covering much of the inner and outer bailey.

The western defences of the castle survive, with the walled motte to the north-west, the gatehouse immediately to the south of it and, at the south-western corner, a circular tower, originally four storeys high and spur buttressed. Beyond it are the remains of a square tower.

The gatehouse, although impressive from outside, is a shell of its former self, with the rear half, which would have contained the accommodation for the constable, long since demolished. What remains is similar to the larger structure at Kidwelly (p. 75), with twin towers and machicolations over the entrance; it was being built at the same time as Kidwelly's gatehouse was under renewed construction, and it would also have had a drawbridge and portcullis, as well as doors.

Carreg Cennen Castle, Carmarthenshire

Ordnance Survey: Landranger 159. *SN: 668 191.*
Entry charge. Guidebook. Cadw.

The position of Carreg Cennen is one of the most impressive in Britain, let alone Wales, especially when viewed at a distance from the south and east. Although a native Welsh castle once stood on this site, the first certain reference to it being in 1248, what we see today mainly dates from the later thirteenth and early fourteenth century and is of English build.

In 1277, during the first Welsh war of King Edward I, the castle was taken by the English. It was eventually given by the Crown to John Giffard, one of the king's men in south Wales, but work on rebuilding the castle does not appear to have begun until after 1284. Giffard died in 1299, and his work was continued by his son John (d.1322). Later in the fourteenth century the castle came into the hands of the Duchy of Lancaster, when some repairs were undertaken, and so passed into Crown possession on the accession of King Henry IV (1399–1413). Damage following its capture by Owain Glyndŵr's supporters resulted in the large sum, in the money of the day, of £500 being expended on refurbishing all parts of the stronghold.

In the Wars of the Roses, in the latter half of the fifteenth century, Carreg Cennen was garrisoned for the house of Lancaster, but was taken by the Yorkists in 1462. Subsequently, some five hundred men were employed over a period of four months to make the castle unusable as a fortress, emphasizing just how strong this castle, built using the hard local limestone, was.

Three building phases are discernible from the masonry, apart from a certain amount of restoration dating to the nineteenth century. The last phase is represented by the footings of the outer ward's defences, with a small twin-towered gateway in the centre of the east wall and solid turrets at the two northern corners. The ward contains the remains of a large limekiln used to make the lime needed for the mortar used in the construction of the walls. From within the ward a ramped barbican led up to the entrance to the inner ward. Even in its ruinous state, it is clear that this was an impressive structure, for anyone wanting to reach the inner gatehouse would not only have had to negotiate a number of 90^0 turns, but halfway up there was a small gatetower, with a stronger version at the top of the barbican; both gates had drawbridges. The barbican was also overlooked by the north-east tower; between this tower and the inner gatehouse the rock-cut ditch may have been used as a cistern for the storage of water.

Spur or angle buttresses, common to several late thirteenth-century English castles in south Wales and the Marches, are a feature of both the north-east tower and the inner gatehouse. The latter's entrance passage was defended by a drawbridge, machicolations, two sets of doors, a portcullis and guard chambers on each side. Inside the inner ward are a number of domestic features. Against the gatehouse are two small tanks or cisterns, and there is also an oven on the west side. Also on this side of the ward is the entrance to the circular north-west tower, one arrowslit in which was converted into a circular gunport in the fifteenth century, to flank the west curtain wall.

On the east side of the ward the domestic range includes a kitchen and a first-floor hall with chambers beyond, as well as a small chapel in the rectangular tower in the centre. In the south-east corner steps lead down to a passage that housed a dovecot, while beyond it a cave runs north under the outer ward.

Cilgerran Castle, Pembrokeshire

Ordnance Survey: Landranger 145. *SN: 195 431.*
Entry charge. Guidebook. Cadw.

Cilgerran, perched on its cliff above the uppermost tidal limit of the river Teifi, has a complicated early history – was this the castle of Cenarth Bychan from which Gerald of Windsor's wife Nest was 'abducted' in an attack in 1109? The first sure mention of Cilgerran as a castle comes with its capture by the Welsh under the Lord Rhys in 1165. The Normans failed to retake the castle, and it was left to the great knight William Marshal (d.1219), who was to carry out so much work at the castles of Chepstow (p. 113) and Pembroke (p. 89), to secure Cilgerran in 1204.

However, during Llywelyn ab Iorwerth's successful campaign in south-west Wales, Cilgerran fell once more into Welsh hands. It was the Marshals' eldest son, another William (d.1231), who finally regained the castle, arriving with a strong force from Ireland in 1223.

He set about its total rebuilding in order to secure its future in Anglo-Norman hands, work which was continued by one or more of his four brothers. However, by 1245 all five men were dead, leaving no male heirs, and, apart from some years when the castle was held by the Crown, Cilgerran passed to the Cantilupe and then the Hastings families until the late fourteenth century, when it passed once more into the hands of the Crown. Cilgerran's castle almost fades from history after that, although it was reported as damaged during the Owain Glyndŵr revolt.

The form of the first castle is unknown, but it may have been a ringwork with timber defences on the site of the inner ward. A fragment of twelfth-century masonry remains near the later inner gatehouse, and this would be in keeping with what the Normans undertook at a number of other castles in the south-west, with stone walls appearing around 1200 at such castles as Kidwelly (p. 75), Laugharne (p. 79) and Llansteffan (p. 82). The securing of the castle in 1223 led to the Marshals initiating a major building programme, leading to the construction of two massive towers, more like keeps than mural towers.

The first tower built was the east tower, and this was soon followed by the enclosing of the outer ward with a stone wall and the outer gate, but only part of this work survives today, the best section, containing a postern gate, abutting the east tower. After the death of William Marshal the younger, one of his brothers continued the work, building the west tower, another outer gatehouse to the west of the earlier one (the latter possibly now being blocked to form a mural tower) and a new inner gate. Parts of the west and north curtain walls of the inner ward also date to the thirteenth century, but the north tower and some of the internal buildings belong to the fourteenth. A number of other medieval buildings survive, although precise dating is not possible. The best lies in the outer ward, by the original outer gate, and appears to have been of timber-framed construction on dwarf stone walls.

The inner gatehouse, which had two upper floors, had a drawbridge and two portcullises, and the approach to it was overlooked by the curtain wall and west tower to the right; note the arrowslits in the curtain wall. The first floor of the gate appears to have been a chapel as it has a piscina or basin in it for washing vessels used in the Mass, unless it had a more utilitarian purpose. The portcullises would also have risen into the chapel, but there are a number of castles where this would have occurred, such as in the King's Gate at Caernarfon (p. 17) and the chapel of Marten's Tower, Chepstow (p. 115).

The two great towers both had three floors over a basement, and one of the other common features that they share is that the outer walls are considerably thicker than the inner. As it was built first, the east tower acted as the castle's keep or main tower, although it was unusual to have a ground-floor entrance to such a tower. However, access to the wall-walk and the upper floors, of which only the topmost had a fireplace, was through a separate ground-floor door and up a spiral staircase. Whereas the upper chamber had a window looking out from the castle, the first- and second-floor rooms had windows overlooking the inner ward. Immediately next to and contemporary with this tower is a small doorway, protected by a portcullis, that led out to the ditch, and thus on to the later postern in the outer curtain.

The west tower, with its first-floor access (the ground-floor doorway and stairs to the next floor were inserted later), became the main tower when it was built. The first and second floors both have fireplaces, as well as windows to the inner ward; such a window is also a feature of the third floor, but there is no fireplace there. Arrowslits covering the ground beyond the inner ward are a feature of the both the east and west towers.

On the west side of the inner ward is the site of the kitchen, and there is also a small limekiln, used in the process for making mortar.

Dinefwr Castle, Carmarthenshire

Ordnance Survey: Landranger 159. *SN: 612 218.*
Guidebook. Cadw.

Unlike Carreg Cennen, with Dinefwr (plate 10; figure 1) and Dryslwyn we have native Welsh castles that have retained their original fabric in spite of later English occupation. These two castles are positioned splendidly in the Tywi valley east of Carmarthen, one of the most picturesque areas of Wales; the strongholds are visible from one other.

Although the earliest phase of masonry dates to the first half of the thirteenth century, a castle was here in the twelfth century, belonging to the princes of south-west Wales, an area known as Deheubarth. The most notable of these princes was the Lord Rhys

(Rhys ap Gruffudd, d.1197), and his court was based at Dinefwr. It was one of his sons, Rhys Gryg (d.1233), who built the five-sided inner ward and the great circular keep at its eastern end. A circular tower was added to the north-west corner a few years later and the main entrance near the south-east corner was strengthened. The original curtain wall on the north-east side has long since collapsed.

After the war of 1277, Dinefwr was held by the English, and considerable rebuilding ensued. In the 1280s the original entrance was replaced by two gateways on the south side of the castle. A third gateway lay to the east, giving access to the outer ward. On the north side of the inner ward a handsome chamber block was erected, against which a hall was added soon after. Thereafter, various small-scale renovations were carried out, including work following the unsuccessful siege in 1403 by the adherents of Owain Glyndŵr. The emphasis of Dinefwr as a residence then shifted to the site now occupied by Newton House, and the medieval castle became a picturesque ruin. The upper part of the keep was converted into a summerhouse in the late seventeenth century, and a new flight of steps built up to the top of the curtain wall by the keep. A porch was also added to the chamber block opposite.

Keeps

The main tower of a castle is often referred to as the keep, although the French word donjon (stemming from the Latin: dominium = lordship) is often used. The first keeps were the small timber towers built on mottes, although soon after the Norman Conquest we have the great towers of London, Colchester in Essex and Chepstow (p. 117) being built. These great towers were constructed not so much for military purposes, but as symbols of lordship designed to overawe and provide the setting for important ceremonies. However, as the siege of Rochester in Kent (1215) showed, a keep was a considerable obstacle for besiegers to overcome in a siege. It was in a generally more peaceful England that the time and resources could be expended to build some of the most lavish keeps of the Middle Ages; in Wales, Norman keeps are much smaller buildings. Most keeps were square or rectangular, but in Wales more round keeps (plate 12) were built than anywhere else in Britain. Another type of keep is known as a shell keep (plate 13), basically a stone curtain wall built around the perimeter of a motte, replacing a timber palisade, with encircling buildings built against the inner face of the wall.

The path to the castle leads through the site of the small English town that replaced an earlier Welsh settlement in the later thirteenth century, and the outer ward with its rock-cut ditch. The visitor passes through the middle gate, overlooked by the keep, past the remains of the original Welsh gate and its steps to the wall-walk, and on to the inner gate, beyond which is a small turret with a chamber and latrine. This turret became another summerhouse in more modern times.

The keep dominates the inner ward, and it is interesting to note that the band of projecting moulded masonry known as a stringcourse that runs between the battered or sloping base and the upper vertical part of the tower is made of Bath stone imported from Somerset. The construction of the summerhouse means that we cannot be certain how many floors the keep had although, in common with most keeps of the Welsh princes, the existing basement and upper storey may have been all that were built. Steps led up to the original first-floor entrance, now blocked; the ground-floor doorway was inserted in the early fourteenth century.

The north-west tower would seem to have been added to the original curtain to serve as a watch tower; its purely military purpose is suggested by the lack of basic amenities such as a fireplace or a latrine. Between this tower and the keep lie the first-floor hall and the chamber block, the building of which resulted in the destruction of the Welsh curtain wall. Presumably the hall replaced an earlier one, the site of which is uncertain. The chamber block had a basement, whilst fine windows and a fireplace, as well as access to a latrine turret, suggest well-appointed accommodation on the ground floor, with even finer apartments on the first floor above.

Dryslwyn Castle, Carmarthenshire

Ordnance Survey: Landranger 159. *SN: 554 204.*
Guidebook. Cadw.

The castle (figure 1) stands on a hill above the river Tywi and until recently all that could be seen were the remains of the chapel tower and a suite of chambers on the south side of the inner ward and, at the opposite end of the castle, the gatehouse to the outer ward. However, excavations from the 1980s have uncovered the plan of the inner ward, including the discovery of a circular keep, and have also shown that the walls were rendered, or covered in mortar, and limewashed to create a startling white appearance.

Dryslwyn's history is similar to Dinefwr's. A castle of the Welsh princes of Deheubarth, it dates from the early thirteenth century, although its first mention in documents is in 1246. One of the Lord Rhys's sons, Rhys Gryg (d.1233), is the most likely candidate for the construction of the earliest masonry – the round keep, curtain wall, hall and chambers in the inner ward at the southern end of the hill. He may have begun the walled enclosure with simple gateway that is the middle ward, unless his son Maredudd (d.1271) undertook this work. The castle was transformed by Maredudd's son, Rhys (d.1292), in the 1280s, seemingly as a reward for his support of the Crown in the Welsh war of 1282–3. Rhys added the outer ward and gatehouse, strengthened the entrance to the inner ward and rebuilt much of that ward's domestic ranges. In other words, Rhys ap Maredudd made Dryslwyn one of the most formidable of all the native Welsh castles built in the thirteenth century.

Rhys rebelled against the Crown in 1287, seemingly unsatisfied with what he saw as limited rewards for his support of the English Crown in 1282–3, as well as being in dispute with local English officialdom. Edmund, earl of Cornwall, England's regent whilst Edward I was abroad, laid siege to the castle with an army of over 11,000 men, and several knights died during the attack. The earl had a trebuchet – a great piece of stone-throwing artillery – constructed on site, and examples of the round stone shot that it hurled were found in the excavations. The castle surrendered after three weeks and was occupied, although Rhys escaped, and repairs were undertaken over the following years. The small Welsh town on the hill, now populated by English burgesses, was also fortified with a wall and gatehouse.

Dryslwyn was taken by the forces of Owain Glyndŵr in 1403, but following its recapture the castle was decommissioned, with doorways and passages being blocked and doors taken down. Later that century the castle was deliberately put to the torch and buildings were demolished so that it could not be used.

A steep climb up the western side of the hill leads the visitor through the remains of the west gatehouse, in front of which was the town ditch, and the hilltop to the north contains the remains of a number of house platforms of the medieval town. The approach to the castle from the late thirteenth century was from the gatehouse to the outer ward, originally reached by a bridge. This two-storeyed structure was blocked up in the fifteenth century, and much of the east side has collapsed. However, enough can be made out to show that the gate passage had two portcullises, as well as doors at the inner end and, presumably, also the outer. A mural staircase runs up the rear of the gate to the upper floor.

Strong walls, barely evident today, ran from the outer gate to enclose the outer ward; a long building was excavated against the western wall. The entrance to the middle ward is simple gateway, but, as this was the outer entrance in the mid-thirteenth century, something more sophisticated may have once existed. A hall was uncovered in this ward during the excavations.

The existing form of the entrance to the core of the castle, the inner ward, dates to Rhys's rebuild of the 1280s. A doorway opened into a passage with a portcullis and a further set of doors at the far end, and there was also a guard chamber to one side. The entrance was overlooked by the great round keep as well, to the left as one stands in the small courtyard. The keep has been demolished to its basement level, and although there is a doorway into the basement, this, like the similarly positioned one at Dinefwr, was a later addition. The main entrance would have been at first-floor level, but whether there was a second floor is unknown, although the Welsh tradition regarding their main towers was just to have one floor above a basement.

Running across the ward is the great hall, which was at first-floor level over a basement, with the great chamber to the left. The huge stone structure in the hall's basement originally supported the central hearth set into the floor of the hall; in front of it stands a fragment of the hall's chimney.

Beyond the great chamber is Rhys's chapel tower, projecting from the early thirteenth-century curtain wall, in which is set a small postern gateway. Between the hall and the south slope of the hill is the suite of private chambers with its view of the river Tywi below.

Other features of the inner ward include a small prison on the west side and a set of latrines on the east, below the round tower.

Haverfordwest Castle, Pembrokeshire

Ordnance Survey: Landranger 157. *SM: 953 157.*
Castle Museum and Record Office.

The castle of medieval Haverford stands in a superb position above the town, on a ridge, with the inner ward, the core of the castle that still stands, overlooking a steep drop on the east side. The castle is first mentioned as late as 1188, but it is likely to have been founded a few decades earlier. It is one of the few castles of the Normans that was never taken by the Welsh.

In the first half of the thirteenth century the Marshal family held the castle. In 1289, for reasons unknown, King Edward I's queen, Eleanor of Castile, acquired it and before her death in November of the following year a considerable sum was spent on the castle; for example, timber felled in Ireland and shipped across cost £360. Most of what survives, apart from a Norman rectangular keep, would appear to date to this time. Haverfordwest largely remained in royal hands from then onwards.

Minor repairs were undertaken in the later Middle Ages, but thereafter it was a case of steady decline. Considerable alterations took place when the castle became a prison in the late eighteenth century. This was replaced by a new gaol in the outer ward in the early nineteenth century, which is now the Pembrokeshire Record Office. The Governor's House, now the town museum, was built around 1780 and occupies the site of the inner gate.

A hall, originally over a vaulted undercroft, occupies the south side of the inner ward; the rounded tower at its south-western corner had a chamber on each of its three floors. A chapel and chamber lie on the east side, between the hall and the keep. A circular tower known as Brechinock stands on the north side, at the junction of the inner and outer wards, and is linked to the keep by a mural passage. Little remains of the outer ward itself and the gatehouse that connected the two wards has totally disappeared.

Kidwelly Castle, Carmarthenshire

Ordnance Survey: Landranger 159. *SN: 409 071*.
Entry charge. Guidebook. Cadw.

Few castles in south Wales are more impressive than Kidwelly (plate 11; figure 9). Built on a scarp above the uppermost navigable limit of the river Gwendraeth, its position close to the sea was typical of many early Norman castles established along the coast of south Wales, as was its original form, a ringwork, as opposed to a motte and bailey.

The castle was founded soon after 1106, the year in which King Henry I (1100–35) gave the Welsh territory of Cydweli to Roger, bishop of Salisbury (d.1139). The castle would have been a large D-shaped ringwork with timber defences, and, as with several other Norman foundations, there were occasions when it was taken and held by the Welsh. The chronicles even record that the Lord Rhys 'built the castle of Cydweli' in 1190, presumably referring to new work done following his capture of it that year. An earlier attack on the castle, in 1136, when it was held by Maurice de Londres, led to the heavy defeat of a Welsh army led by Gwenllian, the wife of Gruffudd ap Rhys of Deheubarth, occasioning her death and that of one son and the capture of another.

The earliest phase of the stone castle dates to around 1200, but whether of Norman or Welsh build one cannot be certain. In comparison with other Norman castles in the area, such as Laugharne (p. 79) and Llansteffan (p. 82), it is likely that the work was undertaken at a time when the Normans had regained control of the castle, either in 1201 or later, in 1220.

The transformation of the castle really began in the later thirteenth century under Payn (d.1279) and Patrick (d.1283) de Chaworth. They were leading lords of the Welsh Marches, and Payn had been with the future King Edward I on crusade in the Holy Land. The new work involved the construction of a square inner ward with four massive towers, the south-east one originally taller than the others. Soon after, the outer curtain wall on the line of the ringwork bank was rebuilt, with four mural towers and a gatehouse to the north and south, so that these two lines of defences formed a concentric castle (p. 124). The new outer defences were heightened not long after, and this necessitated the raising of three of the inner ward towers so that those on the battlements would still have clear views over the now taller outer walls;

the blocked-up original battlements can still be traced in the masonry of the inner ward towers.

In 1283 the castle was acquired by William de Valence, uncle of King Edward I, and it was probably Valence who undertook further work in the inner ward by adding a new kitchen, hall and solar or private chamber, and the handsome chapel, that projects down the slope towards the river.

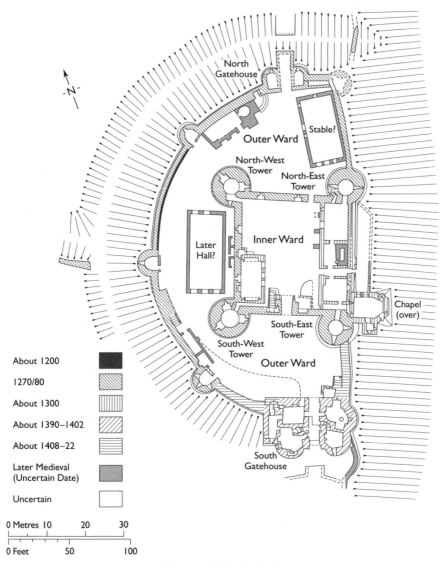

Figure 9: Kidwelly Castle

The castle passed into the hands of the house of Lancaster after the death of Valence in 1296. At the end of the fourteenth century, the castle became an administrative centre for the Duchy of Lancaster and the Chaworth south gate was dismantled to make way for a more imposing structure. The new gate was begun about 1390, but the construction was interrupted by the Owain Glyndŵr revolt, when the castle was besieged in 1403. The castle held out, although the small town within its own circuit of walls and the houses beyond were sacked. Work resumed on the half-built, partly damaged gate from about 1408 and continued until 1422, when the gatehouse was roofed with lead. Two new short stretches of curtain wall ran from it, one wall linking the gate to the first Chaworth mural tower to the west, the other running north to meet the inner ward. The gatehouse also had a new stair turret added in the north-west corner. The cost of the work undertaken after 1408 came to £500.

Later medieval work included two rectangular buildings and a bakehouse in the outer ward, and a malt kiln in the basement of the hall range. At this same time a curving wall was built in front, and to the side, of the great gate as a barbican or outer defence of the main entrance.

The castle is entered through the great gatehouse, a building with some twenty rooms, varying from basement storage rooms or prisons, to guard chambers and fine residential accommodation on the upper floors for the constable and visiting duchy officials. The entrance passage was approached via a drawbridge, and then there was a great two-leaf doorway; this area was further protected by arched murder holes at battlement level. Within, the entrance passage itself had two portcullises, murder holes in the vaulted roof and a second set of doors at the end. Three doors on each side lead into various rooms, the last one on the right as one enters the castle leading into a chamber which looks as if it has a well or prison set into the floor. In fact, this chamber was an office for Duchy of Lancaster officials, and the circular opening in the floor was the only means of access to the strongroom where valuables could be kept.

The original plan to access the upper floors of the gatehouse was to have a central staircase, the half-built remains of which can be seen off the main room at the front of the left or west tower. During the second construction phase, from about 1408, a new stair turret was built from the ground floor upwards at the north-west corner, while the main entrance was constructed against the outside of the rear of the east tower, with a flight of steps leading up to the first floor. The main room on the first floor was the hall and above it was a private apartment or solar. The upper two floors also contained a number of chambers, many with fireplaces and access to latrines. Adjacent to the hall is the kitchen, from which a door leads out to the curtain wall to the inner ward; this affords the visitor the best view of the chapel tower and attached sacristy. The gatehouse was also linked to the outer curtain wall-walk on the west side.

Proceeding round the outer ward one sees that the masonry rear walls of the mural towers on the outer curtain were added at the same time as the curtain was raised; originally, the towers may have been timber-backed. In front of the west wall of the inner ward is a large rectangular building that may have been the great stable or a courthouse; both are known to have existed inside the castle. To one side of the small north gatehouse is the late medieval bakehouse with its massive ovens, whilst on the other lies another rectangular building, possibly a stable.

The inner ward is entered from small gateways in the north and south curtain walls. The enclosure is dominated by the four great corner towers, each of a different design and equipped with a number of chambers, and each having an array of arrowslits. The battlements of the one to the south-west can be reached by the staircase, the top of which ends in a small turret providing a high vantage point for a sentry. The upper rooms of this tower can be entered due to the stone vaulting – elsewhere the floors in the towers were of timber. The western and northern wall-walks are accessible from the external staircase that leads up to this tower. The northern stretch is provided with both front and rear battlements (parapet and parados) and it is evident that defenders would have had to use crossbows rather than longbows in the confined space.

The north-west tower is kidney shaped to the rear due to the presence of a staircase on either side of a recessed upper entrance. The north-east tower, following the construction of the hall and solar became the private residence of the lord of the castle, and certainly in the fifteenth century it had its own private chapel. However, when the towers were first built, the private accommodation for the Chaworth family was in the great south-east tower, with fireplaces on all the upper floors, but later developments relegated this tower to staff use and the lower rooms became service areas.

Little survives of the hall range. The hall would have been on the first floor, and between it and the north-east tower there was a small well-lit private chamber with a fireplace and chimney. Below the hall there would have been room for storage and a wine and ale cellar. Across the inner ward from the hall are the well-preserved remains of a medieval kitchen, lacking only its roof and internal fittings, with a small latrine on the north side. The kitchen has two fireplaces, an oven and a number of cupboards.

One of the glories of the castle is the chapel tower, with great spur buttresses supporting it on its eastern face. The tower has three storeys and the chapel occupies the first floor, as indicated by its windows, sedile or seat for the priest and the small recess to its left, a piscina or basin in which the vessels used in the Mass would have been cleansed. The small stone-roofed building off the south side of the tower was the sacristy, a place where vessels used in the Mass, altar cloths and vestments would have been stored, as confirmed by fifteenth-century records that still survive. The castle chaplain would have resided on the ground floor, but we know that in the later Middle Ages this chamber was being used by a Duchy of Lancaster auditor during his periodic visits, with the basement converted into a strongroom, accessible only from the auditor's room.

The town walls date from the 1280s, and the best section is that on the north, running west from the castle. The ruined rectangular gatehouse at the south end of the small town consists of two towers and a central gate-passage. It had at least one portcullis, although the slot for this was later blocked. The building was described in the sixteenth century as having a town hall on the upper floor, with a prison beneath.

Laugharne Castle, Carmarthenshire

Ordnance Survey: Landranger 159. *SN: 302 107.*
Entry charge. Guidebook. Cadw.

This castle (figure 10) was one of a number founded along the coastline by the Normans in the twelfth century. The first possible reference to it is in 1116 when it was entrusted to a Welshman by the Normans, and the archaeological evidence of the 1976–93 excavations suggests that at that date the castle was probably an earth-and-timber ringwork, like Kidwelly and Llansteffan. The Lord Rhys took the castle, amongst others, in 1189, and at some stage in this period much of the original ringwork enclosure became the outer bailey of the castle. A smaller enclosure was built within it, equivalent to the inner bailey today, and in this new enclosure the excavations revealed that there had been a first-floor stone hall.

Laugharne was regained after 1189 for in 1215 it fell to Llywelyn ab Iorwerth, and the excavations revealed a mass of burning and debris that may relate to this phase of the castle's history. When it was retaken we cannot say, but by 1247 Laugharne was in the hands of the Brian family of Devon, and a succession of lords named Guy de Brian held the lordship until the late fourteenth century; it is their castle that stands preserved today, albeit with sixteenth-century additions.

By the middle of the thirteenth century, two large round towers, a gateway and a domestic range had been constructed. By the end of the century, the gateway had been extended outwards to form a proper gatehouse, the south curtain wall rebuilt and a small tower added at the south-west corner, with a latrine turret adjacent to it. Also, the

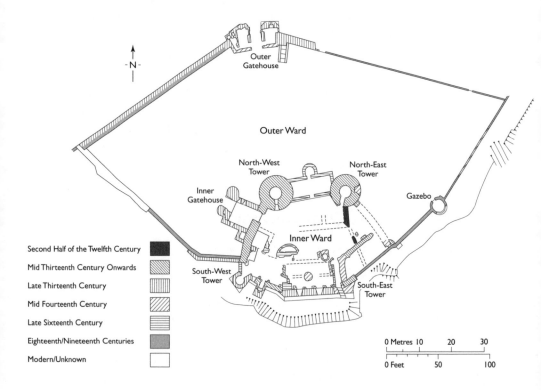

Figure 10: Laugharne Castle

outer bailey's curtain had been constructed and a fine new twin-towered gatehouse added. In the later fourteenth century, the last Guy de Brian heightened the inner gatehouse and the south-west tower, and the domestic range was enhanced. There followed a succession of owners until Sir John Perrot, Queen Elizabeth I's deputy in Ireland, was granted tenancy of the castle in 1575. His occupation resulted in the last main building phase at the castle, when a new range was built between the two northern towers, the inner gate heightened and the hall with its kitchen improved. Perrot may not have fully completed his work at the time of his death in the Tower of London in 1592, but Laugharne had nevertheless been converted into a grand country house, as had Perrot's castle of Carew (p. 63), where a better idea of the scale of Perrot's building works may be obtained.

Laugharne was held by the royalists in the wars of the 1640s, but was taken by the parliamentarians in 1644, the siege and subsequent demolition activities resulting in much damage to the outer gatehouse and other parts of the castle. The outer ward was developed into a garden during the nineteenth century, and Cadw has now restored it along those lines, with paths and planting. In the twentieth century, the castle came to be associated with two authors, Richard Hughes and Dylan Thomas. In 2007, a plaque and arbour were unveiled to commemorate Richard Avent, the excavator of the castle and author of the current guidebook.

The outer gatehouse, with its characteristic late thirteenth-century spur buttresses, consists of a ground floor with a guard chamber on each side, and a chamber above. The earliest work is denoted by the use of red sandstone, the green stone marking a refacing of about 1350. After passing through the gatehouse, the visitor faces the inner ward; from right to left there are the inner gatehouse, the north-west tower, the Elizabethan range with its tall central stair tower and the much ruined north-east tower. The north-west tower was the main tower of the castle and consists of a basement and three upper floors. It has a domed roof, but the battlements were restored in the 1930s. Its sister tower to the north-east had only two floors over a basement.

Even allowing for the heightening of about 1350 and the sixteenth-century alterations, the late thirteenth-century inner gatehouse is a slender structure. When the original simple entrance was converted into a gatehouse and built out over the inner ditch, a basement was created. This was discovered in the excavations, and a doorway or postern led out from this room so that one could reach the foreshore via the ditch and another postern on the shore edge. The original gatehouse had an upper floor, and then in the middle of the fourteenth century the basement was filled in and a second floor was added. Perrot further heightened the gatehouse and added a fine window, now blocked.

On the south side of the inner ward lay the hall range and kitchen, the hall being at first-floor level. The large opening looking out to sea marks the site of Perrot's oriel window and next to it is the fireplace, with its chimney above.

Llandovery Castle, Carmarthenshire

Ordnance Survey: Landranger 146. *SN: 767 342.* **Local authority.**

There is enough remaining of the castle on the south side of the town, by the car park, to show that in its original form it was an earth-and-timber motte and bailey, first mentioned in 1116. The motte was created by scarping a natural knoll that overlooks the river Brân. The chronicles mention the castle on numerable occasions, Llandovery being taken and retaken by both the Normans and the Welsh.

Its recapture from the Welsh in the war of 1282–3 led to the castle's being strengthened by the addition of a D-shaped main tower, and there are also the remains of a twin-towered gatehouse and other walling.

Llansteffan Castle, Carmarthenshire

Ordnance Survey: Landranger 159. *SN: 351 101.*
Guidebook. Cadw.

This castle stands in a prominent position overlooking the entrance to the Tywi estuary and was built on the site of an Iron Age fort, the banks of which can still be seen on the west side. The defensive possibilities of the site were fully understood by the Normans, engaged as they were in the construction of a chain of castles on or close to the coast in south-west Wales.

In 1146 the chronicles record not only a successful Welsh attack on the castle, but a successful defence of it, when the Welsh threw down the ladders used by the Normans in an attempt to scale the palisade.

This is the first mention of the castle, although it is likely it had been founded some decades earlier.

As with so many of its companions, it fell to the Lord Rhys in 1189 and fell again in 1215, this time to Llywelyn ab Iorwerth. Regained in 1223, it remained in English hands thereafter, mainly in the hands of the de Camville family until the early fourteenth century, apart from a short-term loss in 1257 and during the Owain Glyndŵr uprising, when the Welsh held it in 1405–6. It was the de Camvilles who radically strengthened the site in the later thirteenth century. The Crown held the castle from the late Middle Ages, and King Henry VII (1485–1509) gave it to his uncle Jasper Tudor, earl of Pembroke (d.1495); it may have been Jasper who undertook the final modifications. Thereafter, the castle ceased to be significant and took on a more agricultural function.

In the later thirteenth century a great twin-towered gatehouse was built as the entrance to the lower ward, similar to the inner east gatehouse at Caerphilly (p. 105) – could it even pre-date Caerphilly? However, its entrance passage was blocked in the late fifteenth century or later, and a new entrance with an upper room built alongside it. Beyond it is the large D-shaped north tower, and this structure and the original gatehouse provide a powerful defensible front to the main approach to the castle.

The great gatehouse had a central vaulted entrance passage with guard chambers on each side, and there were two portcullises and a series of murder holes, best appreciated by standing on the first floor above. On the exterior face, above the later blocking, there are the remains of a chute, possibly for water to be poured down should the original wooden doors have been set alight. Caerphilly's inner east gate has a similar chute in its rear wall. To reach the gatehouse's two upper rooms one had to pass through the passage into the lower ward and proceed up steps on the west side to the first-floor doorway; the spiral staircases in the rear turrets led up to the second floor and battlements, the eastern one also giving access to latrines. The large fireplace and windows indicate a room of some pretension on the first floor, perhaps the lord's hall, with an equally fine but more private room on the second floor, again with windows and a large fireplace. The handsome corbels that supported the hood of the upper fireplace are very evident, as are the carved stone brackets on each side to support lamps.

The north tower has a basement with its own doorway, but the main entrance was at first-floor level, opening on to a small landing and on to a chamber, with a newel staircase leading up to the second floor. With its own latrine, this tower must have provided additional private accommodation for the lords of the castle; both rooms had windows and fireplaces. Between this tower and the range in the east corner there was a large Tudor barn, possible on the site of the medieval hall. The so-called east bastion with its loop and latrines may have formed part of the hall complex. On the other, west, side of the lower ward there is a smaller and somewhat damaged D-shaped tower; it had a single arrowslit on the ground floor, but the upper floor provided additional accommodation, there being a fireplace and a latrine.

Moving up to the inner ward, the curtain wall of about 1200 survives on the west side, heightened and supported by a series of vaults in the late thirteenth century. Early in the thirteenth century a gatetower was built, with a portcullis and two upper chambers, that on the first floor accessible from the wall-walk. At the same time as this gate was built a round tower was added on the east side, the footings of which, as well as a number of other buildings of uncertain date, were uncovered in excavations in the 1960s and 1970s.

Llawhaden Castle, Pembrokeshire

Ordnance Survey: Landranger 158. *SN: 073 175.*
Guidebook. Cadw.

In its current, largely late fourteenth-century form, Llawhaden is more a grand ecclesiastical mansion of the bishops of St Davids than a castle. However, it was as an earth-and-timber castle ringwork that it began life, probably founded by the Norman Bishop Bernard in the early twelfth century. It was one of the many castles captured (in 1192) and destroyed (in 1193) by the Lord Rhys. At some stage in the early thirteenth century the castle was rebuilt in stone, although the only evidence for this is the remains of some round towers and part of the curtain wall. Either at the same time or later in that century, a square latrine tower was added, now behind the east tower of the present gatehouse.

The castle was transformed in the late fourteenth century by Bishop Adam de Houghton. Most of this work was finished by 1383, although it is thought that the new gatehouse may date to a few years later. This structure, the latrine and chapel towers, as well as the lodgings range, gave Llawhaden a martial appearance. However, the new buildings were more for show and status, and provided suites of handsome and comfortable accommodation, as well as service ranges that included a kitchen and, later, a bakehouse. This was the last phase in the castle's history, for after the sixteenth-century Reformation it fell into decline.

Passing an animal pound on the left, possibly dating to the eighteenth century, one enters through the ruined, but majestic spur-buttressed, twin-towered gatehouse. Originally, there would have been a drawbridge, and over the entrance passage there were once machicolations or murder holes, a feature seen at Carmarthen (p. 65) and Kidwelly (p. 77). The passage, in common with other gatehouses, had a portcullis, as well as doors. The rooms in the gatehouse provided good accommodation, several of the vaulted chambers being well lit and having fireplaces, and it is presumed that the bishop's constable and his family would have resided here. The earlier tower, incorporated into the new gatehouse, continued to provide the latrine facilities.

The bishop's accommodation lay in the hall range on the far side of the castle as one enters the courtyard. His hall lay on the first floor, with a private chamber at the same level in the south cross-wing. The northern cross-wing contained service rooms. On the ground floor of the hall range and cross-wings were vaulted undercrofts used for storage. Extending westwards from the northern cross-wing are the remains of the later medieval bakehouse.

The south range, originally connected to the hall block by a short stretch of curtain wall, contained the chapel and the accommodation for the bishop's household and guests, built over vaulted undercrofts. The main access to this range was via a tall, slender five-storey porch, its ground-floor doorway being flanked by two fine carved heads. There were small chambers on the upper floors. Being the tallest building in the castle, the porch tower would have had views over the entire castle and the immediate hinterland.

The chapel is on the first floor, with a polygonal tower projecting from it. The tower had a prison in its basement and a mural latrine on the ground floor. The chamber on the tower's first floor may have served as either accommodation for a priest, as there is a fireplace and a latrine, or a sacristy to house the Mass vessels. The vaulted room above is even finer, but may have served an administrative purpose. The main windows of the accommodation range overlooked the courtyard. There were two main chambers, two on the first floor and two on the second, and they all had fireplaces. In an arrangement similar to that in the Fountain Court at Raglan (p. 137), mid way along the outside of the south range there was a latrine or closet tower, although at Llawhaden this tower also contained small bedchambers. A smaller accommodation block was built against one of the gatehouse towers and the early thirteenth-century round tower.

Manorbier Castle, Pembrokeshire

Ordnance Survey: Landranger 158. *SS: 065 978.*
Entry charge. Guidebook. Private trust.

Gerald of Wales (d.1223), of Norman and Welsh descent, described the area around Manorbier, his birthplace, as 'the most pleasant place by far' in all of Wales, and it is hard to disagree. For students of early castle architecture the castle is a delight as it dates to the late twelfth century through to the later thirteenth century. In other words, the later centuries have had little impact on this site, apart from the sixteenth- or seventeenth-century barn and the modern house in the inner ward.

The castle was involved little in national events, and it seems to have led a peaceful existence under the de Barri family from the time of its first mention (1146) until the fourteenth century. In various ownership thereafter, including the Crown, it was fortified in the civil war, but mainly seems to have served an agricultural function from the end of the Middle Ages. In 1880, the antiquary J. R. Cobb acquired the castle and, as well as restoring some floors in two of the towers, he built the house just inside the inner gate. Cobb also undertook work at Pembroke and Caldicot castles (pp. 90, 107).

The outer ward still has some traces of the medieval curtain and towers, but it is dominated by a ruinous post-medieval barn. This barn cuts into a stone-revetted earthwork, added in the 1640s during the civil war to provide extra defences to the gatehouse; this earthwork is comparable to those at Carew (p. 63) and Newcastle Emlyn (p. 89).

The gatehouse area has structures of a range of medieval dates, whilst the curtain wall on either side shows signs of being heightened at various times, the original battlements being 'fossilized' within the masonry. To the right of the gatehouse is the shell of the 'old tower', dating to the late twelfth century and so, along with the hall at the far end of the site, contemporary with Gerald of Wales himself. It is assumed that this tower overlooked the original entrance, but this was rebuilt in the early thirteenth century. Later in the same century the existing gatehouse was built, with an outer portcullis; an inner portcullis may have been retained from the slightly earlier entrance, if indeed a portcullis was still set here at this date. The gatehouse has two upper rooms, reached from the round tower to the south, the uppermost being well lit and having a fireplace, as well as a latrine projecting out over the ditch.

Most of the original curtain wall, like the towers on either side of the gatehouse, dates to the early thirteenth century, as does the guard chamber between the gatehouse and the round tower. The curtain that enclosed the extreme western end of the castle has long since disappeared. Against the north curtain at the far end of the inner ward are various ovens that imply the kitchens were in this area, and then we have the most interesting part of Manorbier, the domestic complex comprising the hall range and the chapel.

Over a number of basement rooms is a handsome late twelfth-century Norman hall, its entrance being at first-floor level. The hall has a fireplace, although the circular chimney is a later replacement, and a wall would have originally separated this room from a small room to the west, above which was the lord's own chamber or solar reached by a stair in the hall. The solar has a fireplace and a short mural passage leads to a latrine. At the junction between the curtain wall and the solar there is another latrine, presumably for the use of those on the walls, as well as the household staff in the service range.

A later thirteenth-century chamber was added to the east of the hall, over the passage to the water gate below, and linked the hall range to the chapel. This chamber gave access to the spur wall, the main function of which was to be a covered passage leading to a latrine. Another door from the chamber opened into the chapel added around 1250, but there was also a more public doorway reached by an external staircase. The chapel, built over a barrel-vaulted basement, also has a barrel vault. It clearly had a series of fine windows originally. Other features include a sedile or priest's chair and traces of wall paintings. Fireplaces were added later to the chapel and the room below, probably in the sixteenth century.

Narberth Castle, Pembrokeshire

Ordnance Survey: Landranger 158. *SN: 110 144.* Local authority.

The recently conserved fragmentary remains of this late thirteenth-century castle are enough to indicate that Narberth, a stronghold of the Mortimer family, was once an impressive fortress. It is likely to have been built after 1257, the year in which Llywelyn ap Gruffudd swept through west Wales destroying several castles, including the earlier castle at Narberth. The new castle consisted of a rectangular courtyard with a massive round tower at each corner, of which the one at the south-west survives best. The north-east tower was larger than the other three, so at Narberth we have a similar building history to that of the almost contemporaneous inner ward at Kidwelly (p. 75), although at Narberth there may have been towers midway along the east and west curtain walls. By the fifteenth century much of the castle was in decay, but an idea of how the castle was arranged is provided in a survey of 1539.

There may have been an outer ward to the castle on the north (town) side. A gatehouse originally stood between the two north towers. A small section of the north-east tower stands to three storeys, and there probably was a fourth. Fireplaces and latrines are evident, and against it is a rectangular structure that may have housed steps leading to a first-floor entrance. To the south of this tower are the remains of a vaulted rectangular building, originally with a great chamber on the first floor, as well as a solar. The south-east tower, of three storeys, may have enclosed a bakehouse at basement level, with a chapel on the first floor. The hall, which seems to have been slightly later than the towers, stood between the two south towers, and a kitchen may have been in the basement. More survives of the three-storey south-west tower than its fellows. It has a number of windows, but if it had fireplaces, evidence for these has now disappeared.

Newcastle Emlyn Castle, Carmarthenshire

Ordnance Survey: Landranger 145. *SN: 311 407.* Local authority.

Although this castle above the river Teifi has a long history, little survives apart from the fourteenth-century inner gatehouse, the upper windows in which date to alterations in the early sixteenth century by Sir Rhys ap Thomas. The remains of a tower to the south of the gate may also be fourteenth century.

The castle of Emlyn may have been a Welsh foundation toward the end of the first half of the thirteenth century, built by a descendant of the Lord Rhys, Maredudd, who also held Dryslwyn Castle (p. 72). The castle came into the possession of the Crown after the Rhys ap Maredudd revolt in 1287 and was retained until the mid-fourteenth century. The royal accounts describe a number of buildings situated in the two wards or baileys. Over £60 was spent on the completion of the inner ward's gatehouse in 1347–8, as well as adjacent buildings and a drawbridge. Thereafter, the castle passed into private hands.

In the civil war of the 1640s the castle was held by both sides at different times. The castle's defences were supplemented with an earthwork known as a redan – to accommodate cannon and musketeers – on the approach to the inner gatehouse. A similar outwork can be seen at Carew (p. 63) and Manorbier (p. 86).

Pembroke Castle, Pembrokeshire

Ordnance Survey: Landranger 158. *SM: 982 016.*
Entry charge. Guidebook. Trust.

There has been a castle at Pembroke since the 1090s, founded by Earl Roger of Shrewsbury when he moved from his centre of power in the middle of the Welsh Marches into south-west Wales. The castle appears to have been an earth-and-timber construction until the early thirteenth century, with a palisaded rampart cutting off the neck of the headland on which it sits. Unlike other Norman castles of the period in west Wales, the Welsh never took this stronghold.

The castle was to pass from the house of Montgomery to the Crown and then into the possession of the Clares, who were granted the earldom of Pembroke in 1138. It was Richard de Clare, known as Strongbow, who became, at the invitation of the king of Leinster, involved with matters in Ireland – an involvement which was the cue for Anglo-Norman occupation of much of that island. Strongbow's daughter and heir, Isabella, had married William Marshal in 1189 and soon thereafter we see William transforming the fortress of Chepstow, with a new gatehouse and mural towers (p. 113). However, the transformation of Pembroke came a few years later, for William's involvement in Normandy until its loss to the English Crown in 1204 meant that it was only then that he could turn his attention to Pembroke.

Marshal was earl of Leinster as well as Pembroke, so the castle and town remained an important stepping stone on the route between Wales and Ireland. Marshal and his sons built a brand new castle on the site, the size of the great round keep making it one of the greatest of such structures to survive in Europe, if not the greatest. When the Marshal male line died out in 1245, Pembroke passed to the Valences, who continued the building of the castle, and then on to a number of different owners. The decline in importance of the castle was halted when it came into the hands of Jasper Tudor in 1454; he made some alterations and additions and, of course, it was at this time, in 1457, that the future King Henry VII (1485–1509), Jasper's nephew, was born within the castle's walls. Following Jasper's death in 1495, Pembroke's castle played no further role in national affairs until the civil war of the 1640s.

Pembrokeshire was a bastion of parliamentary support, unlike the rest of Wales, and the castle was strengthened by the town's formidable mayor, John Poyer. Nevertheless, discontent led Poyer to declare for the king in 1648 and it was Oliver Cromwell himself who was sent to take the castle, which he duly did after a short siege. As a result, the castle and town walls were slighted, gunpowder being employed to destroy many of the castle's towers. The appearance of the castle today owes much to the restoration of the towers in the nineteenth and twentieth centuries, completed in the 1930s.

The great castle historian, David Cathcart King (d.1989), assigned the construction of the inner and outer wards, as well as the town walls, to William Marshal. Many scholars were uneasy about dating such a massive programme of works to Marshal, even if it was continued by his sons, and the outer ward is now interpreted as the work of William de Valence around the middle of the thirteenth century.

The entrance to the castle is through the restored barbican. The barbican was later than the gatehouse, its construction removing the need for the original drawbridge that is said to have existed over a ditch. The three-storeyed gatehouse is unusual in plan for the western half has the usual D-shaped tower, while the eastern half is a plain rectangular block. However, immediately beyond it, and overlooking the approach to the castle, is the circular Barbican Tower, and this compensates for the gatehouse not being a twin-towered structure. The gatehouse passage, in common with its contemporaries, was defended by portcullises, doors, arrowslits, guard chambers and machicolations. The chambers on the upper floors, three on each level, provided accommodation. A wall across the upper level of the rear of the building, between the stair turrets, was built later, seemingly as an additional defence.

The curtain wall from the Barbican Tower runs to meet the round Northgate Tower, the town wall originally meeting the castle at this point, and so on round to the St Anne's Bastion, an additional defence added in the early fourteenth century, with a postern gate by it. The curtain wall, with three mural towers, west of the outer gatehouse runs round to butt against the inner ward. Between the gatehouse and the Westgate Tower, and running round the rear of the Henry VII Tower, the inner face of the curtain has been reinforced in stone, and this was undertaken by Poyer in the 1640s in order to reinforce the wall against artillery fire.

The Monkton Tower, which did not suffer in the post-1648 destruction, overlooks another postern. The tower has two floors with no connection between them. The lower is reached via a passage on the south side, off which is a small chamber with medieval graffiti, whilst the upper room can be entered only from the wall-walk on the north side.

The entrance to the inner ward is through the Horseshoe Gate, of which only the footings remain. The entrance passage is placed in the flank of the tower, and a similar and better surviving arrangement can be seen at Caldicot Castle (p. 109). The inner ward is dominated by William Marshal's massive circular keep, begun soon after 1204. Four storeys high, with an attic under a domed roof, it offered little in the way of domestic comfort apart from fireplaces on two of the floors. The doorway into the basement must be late medieval, for the original entrance, as one would expect, is at first-floor level, with a restored newel staircase leading up to the other floors. A narrow doorway on the second floor appears to have given access to the wall-walk via a wooden bridge. The keep has a number of arrowslits, as well as windows on the principal floors, and the roof level would have been enclosed by a projecting timber hourd or gallery that would have allowed the keep's defenders to command the foot of the wall.

The Dungeon Tower and North Turret form part of the inner ward's defences, but, where the original early thirteenth-century curtain survives, it is only a thin wall; Marshall relied on the natural defences that the site provided at this point. Abutting the Dungeon Tower on the outside of the curtain wall is a latrine block of the later thirteenth century. Backing on to this block is a small solar or private chamber notable for its chimney stack. This room once had a fine oriel window overlooking the inner ward, added by Jasper Tudor.

The early domestic buildings lie on the west side of the inner ward and consist of a narrow hall or chamber and a chapel. The other domestic buildings, as well as the water gate situated in the cave known as the Wogan, lie on the east side of the inner ward. There are the remains of a later twelfth-century first-floor hall, possibly the only masonry in an otherwise timber castle. Alongside it is the late thirteenth-century hall overlooking the water, the hall again being on the first floor, with the kitchen beneath it. The hall was served by another latrine block, but this pre-dates the hall, belonging to the Marshal period.

Chapels

The chapel was an important building in a castle and some castles contained more than one, with the main chapel being for the use of the constable and garrison and a smaller, private one – an oratory – for the lord or the king, as at Conwy (p. 25). Clues to a room's use as a chapel come from the remains of sedile or seat for the priest and the piscina, a wall basin in which the vessels would have been washed after the Mass.

A chapel may have been freestanding in the castle's bailey or built as part of the main structure. At Kidwelly (plate 11) a tower was built down the steep gradient towards the river with the chapel on the upper storey (p. 79) and at Beaumaris one of the great mural towers was the chapel (p. 14) (plate 3). At both Beaumaris and Conwy there were closets or small chambers from which the king could observe the Mass in private.

The larger gatehouses also incorporated chapels and oratories, but as these were often placed on the first floor and above the entrance passage, it was not unusual to have the inconvenience of one or more portcullises raised into the rooms. Such a feature can be seen in the King's Gate at Caernarfon (p. 17) and at Harlech (p. 37), whilst the portcullis protecting the wall-walk on one side of Marten's Tower at Chepstow (p. 115) would also have been raised into the private chapel. This may suggest that at most times of the day a castle's portcullis remained lowered.

The other main remains in the inner ward are of a rectangular building called the Chancery, added in the late thirteenth century. From here administrative and legal matters relating to the earldom would have been undertaken.

Running in an easterly direction from the castle is the elongated medieval town of Pembroke, once fully enclosed by walls, although the date of construction is uncertain – perhaps later thirteenth century. These defences are now fragmentary, but traces of the curtain wall, gates and towers can be seen. One tower on the south side is being used as a gazebo, whilst close to it is another circular tower.

However, the most remarkable structure, perhaps unique in British urban defences, is Barnard's Tower, which stands at the north-east corner of the walled circuit, overlooking the northern and eastern approaches to the town. This appears to have been a self-contained three-storeyed defensive residence with a drawbridge. The tower has a number of arrowslits, a newel staircase and windows, including two in the topmost chamber; this room also has a fireplace.

St Clears Castle (Banc y Beili), Carmarthenshire

Ordnance Survey: Landranger 158. *SN: 281 154.* Open access.

Set in a playground, this castle is a fine example of a motte and bailey, although the ditches that would have surrounded both have long since been infilled.

A Norman priory was founded here around 1100, which would suggest that a castle already stood here. The castle was held by both the Normans and the Welsh at different times in the twelfth and thirteenth centuries. It appears to have survived into the fifteenth century, when it was besieged, and possibly captured, by the forces of Owain Glyndŵr. Such a lengthy history suggests that, although no masonry is evident, the castle's original timber defences may have been wholly or partly replaced in stone. Possible confirmation of this comes from a late seventeenth-century comment that digging on the top of the motte had yielded stone and mortar.

Tenby Castle and town walls, Pembrokeshire

Ordnance Survey: Landranger 158. *SN: 137 005.* **Local authority.**

The headland known as Castle Hill supports the very fragmentary remains of the castle. Although there was a castle here in the twelfth century, the masonry represents its later thirteenth-century phase, but there are precious few features to provide an accurate date.

A D-shaped barbican acts as the outer defence of a square gateway, and there is a short stretch of curtain wall with arrowslits. On the highest point of the interior there is a watchtower formed from a square and a circular tower. Elsewhere, odd bits of medieval walling do not really help to provide a picture of the castle in the Middle Ages.

Whereas the castle is fragmentary, the same cannot be said of the town walls, and they are of particular interest in that they have some of the few examples of medieval gunloops in Wales, probably dating to the 1450s. The circuit of the walls was originally far more extensive than it is today; the short stretch from the site of the north gate to the north-west corner and the wall running south from this corner down to the cliff edge are the main survivals.

The original defences consisted of an earth bank and palisade, but the masonry wall was added later, probably some time in the thirteenth century. Some of the towers were added later, in the early fourteenth century and when Jasper Tudor strengthened the defences from 1457. He heightened walls and towers, provided additional arrowslits and made a new wall-walk.

One of the best-known features of the circuit is the Five Arches. This is a D-shaped barbican built to protect the south gate in the 1320s. One of the 'arches' is the original entrance, with portcullis slot, but the other four are modern enlargements of what must have been arrowslits originally. The rectangular tower to the south of the Five Arches dates to the late fifteenth century, and its gunloops at first-floor level are of the inverted keyhole type – a form to be seen earlier in several castles and town walls in southern England in the late fourteenth century, a time of increasing threats of French raids.

Wiston Castle, Pembrokeshire

One would have to travel far to see a better example of a motte-and-bailey castle than Wiston, coupled with the fact that the motte still supports a good example of a shell keep.

The castle was founded in the early twelfth century by a man called Wizo, one of the many Flemings who accompanied the Normans in their settlement of south-west Wales. Wizo may have made use of an existing, prehistoric, earthwork known as a rath for the bailey, on one side of which he built the motte. As with so many other castles in Wales, its history is one of Welsh capture and loss. It is known that the Welsh took it in 1147, 1193 and 1220, when it was destroyed by Llywelyn ab Iorwerth. King Henry III (1216–72) ordered the castle to be rebuilt soon after, and it is possible that the shell keep on the summit of the motte dates to this time, when it was in the hands of the Marshal family.

The masonry of the keep is built in a series of straight lengths, and its doorway was secured by a drawbar, the socket of which remains. The flight of steps is slightly later than the shell keep, and these steps with the two walls projecting into the interior suggest a first-floor hall or chamber. There must also have been access to the shell keep's wall-walk. The wall built against the inner face of the keep is also of a later phase.

Some small-scale archaeological work undertaken in the 1990s uncovered evidence that the castle remained occupied until at least the middle of the fourteenth century.

6

The South-East
(Breconshire, Glamorgan and Monmouthshire)

Abergavenny Castle, Monmouthshire

Ordnance Survey: Landranger 161. *SO: 299 139.* Local authority.

Little survives of this castle, the centre of the lordship of Abergavenny and one of the more important strongholds of the Welsh Marches. It stands on raised ground overlooking the river Usk, a little distance away to the south. The motte of the castle, raised in the late eleventh century by Hamelin de Ballon, survives, on top of which is a building of 1819, built by the earl of Abergavenny and now part of the town's museum. Most of the masonry dates to the thirteenth and fourteenth centuries, when the lordship was held by such major families as the Braose and the Hastings families.

The gateway to the castle is a relatively unimpressive late medieval building, with a passage that was originally vaulted and an upper floor containing a fireplace and window. The main section of curtain wall that survives, against part of which stood the hall, runs from the gatehouse. Overlooking the low ground to the south is a pair of differently shaped conjoined towers, in the manner of Crickhowell (p. 122); here, one is round and the other polygonal, with a latrine turret adjacent. Although only the external walls survive, enough remains to show that these towers stood four storeys high.

Barry Castle, Glamorgan

Ordnance Survey: Landranger 171. *ST: 101 672.* Local authority.

A mere shadow of its former glory, the castle or fortified manor of Barry today consists of a fourteenth-century gatehouse and part of a slightly later hall range alongside it. Both were part of a rebuilding of a now largely vanished thirteenth-century stronghold that had, in its turn, replaced a Norman fortification, possibly a ringwork. The gatehouse had a portcullis which was operated from a room on the upper floor that may have also been a chapel, and which also communicated with the hall to its west.

Bridgend (Newcastle), Glamorgan

Ordnance Survey: Landranger 170. *SS: 902 801.* Guidebook. A key needs to be obtained to enter the castle. Cadw.

Although a royal castle had been established at Cardiff by 1081 (p. 110), it was to be from Gloucester that Robert fitz Hamon and other Normans moved west across Glamorgan in the closing years of the eleventh century. The Vale of Glamorgan marked the extent of this preliminary Norman advance, the river Ogmore providing the initial boundary. Three castles were founded on this western limit: the new castle at Bridgend, Coity (p. 118) and Ogmore itself (p. 129). Bridgend may have been built by fitz Hamon by around 1106, and later in the twelfth century it was held by two earls of Gloucester, Robert (d.1147) and his son William (d.1183).

Newcastle Bridgend stands on a bluff over the river Ogmore and is unusual in that it has little later medieval masonry – most of what can be seen today is Norman. Apart from refurbishment of the main domestic building in the bailey, the hall, Newcastle remained largely unaltered until the sixteenth century, when new windows were added to the south tower.

The castle may well have started as a ringwork, but at some time in the twelfth century a keep was added, the existence of which was reported in the nineteenth century. This addition may have been made at the same time as the curtain wall and the mural towers were built, in the 1180s. The construction of mural towers in the late twelfth century is rare, certainly in Wales, but can be seen at Dover and a few other castles in England. The builder may have been King Henry II (1154–89) himself, who held the castle after a Welsh uprising in 1183–4 until his death. The only other possible builder is Earl William of Gloucester.

The entrance to the castle is through a handsome Norman gateway in the lee of the square south tower. The door opening is framed by notable carved decoration, some of the best Norman work in

Glamorgan outside church architecture. The entrance still has some of the fine-quality ashlar masonry framing it, although elsewhere in the castle this ashlar has been robbed for reuse locally. The main features in the south tower – the doorways, windows and a basement fireplace – are Tudor, but on the first floor, accessed by an external stair, a Norman fireplace survives, and in the remains of the second floor another medieval fireplace is visible.

The foundations of the building on the right as one enters the courtyard are all that remain of an early Norman hall, whilst those beyond it belong to a structure of the thirteenth century. Traces of another building of unknown date lie to the north, whilst on the west side is another square mural tower.

Bronllys Castle, Breconshire

Ordnance Survey: Landranger 161. *SO: 148 347.* Cadw.

The original castle was an earth-and-timber motte with two baileys (the latter are in a privately owned area), but in the early thirteenth century the circular keep was built on the summit of the motte (plate 12). The castle is likely to have been built in the late eleventh or early twelfth century, when further inroads into this area were made by the Normans.

Bronllys came into the possession of the Clifford family, and it was probably the third Walter de Clifford (d.1263), rather than the second of that name (d.1221), who built the great keep that we see today. Walter III is a good example of an Anglo-Norman lord who married into a Welsh dynastic house, for his wife was the daughter of Llywelyn ab Iorwerth, prince of Gwynedd. Bronllys passed to John Giffard, who rebuilt Carreg Cennen (p. 66), after he married Walter's daughter, but around 1311 it came into the hands of a Welshman, Rhys ap Hywel, a member of a family who served the Marcher lords, as well as the Crown. At some stage in the early fourteenth century the uppermost floor of the round keep was added, or perhaps totally rebuilt, and windows were altered on the lower floors; this work was undertaken either by Rhys or his son Philip.

Late in the fourteenth century Bronllys was acquired by that great Marcher family, the Bohuns, lords of Brecon, while during the following century it was held by the Crown, and gradually fell into decay, apart from being repaired during the Glyndŵr uprising.

The keep would have been approached from the bailey originally, with a staircase leading up to the first-floor entrance. When the keep was first built there was a wooden floor over the basement, but in the later Middle Ages a stone vault replaced the original timber. The basement was reached by a flight of steps from one of two windows lighting the entrance foyer. In the side of the second window embrasure a staircase leads up to the second floor. This floor, the level of which was altered at some date, has windows, later themselves altered with new, pointed, openings, and there is also a fireplace. However, there is no latrine at this level; this is found on the topmost floor, the most private of rooms, together with three windows and a fireplace. If the third floor is indeed an addition, as opposed to a rebuild, in the early fourteenth century, it would appear that Rhys ap Hywel or his son required a better standard of accommodation in the castle's main tower, even to the extent of remodelling the windows.

Although it has long since vanished, eighteenth-century prints of Bronllys depict a large hall block in the inner bailey, as one would have expected.

Builth Castle, Breconshire

Ordnance Survey: Landranger 147. *SO: 044 510.* Local authority.

The castle is one of the most impressive motte and baileys in Wales, and the other point of interest is that it was refortified by King Edward I following the Welsh war of 1277. Little is known about this later phase apart from some documentation, for the masonry has been robbed over the centuries, and the visitor is left with only the earthworks to examine.

The castle was built in the late eleventh or early twelfth century by the Braose family, in a commanding position overlooking the river Wye. Like so many other castles, it was taken by the Welsh in the twelfth century. The Braose family recovered it, but then lost it to King John (1199–1216), who refortified it. The castle passed into the hands of Llywelyn ab Iorwerth through the marriage of his son, Dafydd, to a Braose heiress, but it was once again in English possession from the 1240s, and it may have been at this time that masonry defences were first built. Acquiring it in 1260, Llywelyn ap Gruffudd held it until it was taken in the first Welsh war.

Following its capture Edward I built a new structure on the motte from 1277, and part of the bailey was cut off; the reduced area was defended by a curtain wall and towers, upon which work continued until 1282. The tower on the motte may have been a shell keep, rather than a great circular tower, for the records mention buildings within it. Documents refer to repairs in the early fourteenth century, and it is clear that even by 1343 the gatehouse had not been finished. From then on the history of the castle is one of abandonment and decline, apart from some minor repairs made in 1409.

Caerleon Castle, Monmouthshire

Ordnance Survey: Landranger 171. *ST: 341 903.* Open access.

Although the large late eleventh-century motte lies in a private garden, well screened from view by a high wall, a later mural tower of the castle survives. Equipped with arrowslits, it was built by William Marshal in the early thirteenth century. It stands in the grounds of the public house, the Hanbury Arms, overlooking the river Usk.

Caerphilly Castle, Glamorgan

Ordnance Survey: Landranger 171. *ST: 155 871.*
Entry charge. Guidebook. Cadw.

Caerphilly (figure 11) is a veritable giant amongst castles, and it is generally regarded as the largest ruined castle in Britain, taking into account the outworks and water defences. The castle is interesting for a number of reasons: the impressive masonry defences, which few European castles can match; the utilization of water on a grand scale as part of its defence, as well as to highlight its imposing architecture; the enlightened conservation, for its day, when parts were rebuilt in the early twentieth century.

The castle was built by the formidable Gilbert de Clare, earl of both Gloucester and Hertford (d.1295), one of the most important lords of the time of King Henry III and his son and successor Edward I, and was established in a politically sensitive area. In terms of wealth and political importance, Gilbert was considered to be second only to the royal family. The part of the lordship of Glamorgan in which the castle was built was the Welshry, for the Normans had made few inroads into the uplands north of Cardiff, and were content not to do so, depending on the political situation. Gilbert's grandfather and father had done much to wrest areas of Glamorgan from Welsh control, but it was the rise of Llywelyn ap Gruffudd and his attempt to assert his authority in the Welshry that must have led Gilbert to embark on the construction of this massive stronghold in 1268. Yet, within a few years, Llywelyn was dead (in 1282) and the threat from the house of Gwynedd came to an end.

Llywelyn had been recognized as prince of Wales by the English Crown in 1267 in the Treaty of Montgomery, and the prince was entitled to the homage of all the Welsh lords. However, in order to protect Cardiff and lowland south-east Glamorgan, Gilbert moved north to dispossess the Welsh lord and began to construct Caerphilly in April 1268, a veritable fortress-palace that became the Clare principal residence. Llywelyn considered this contrary to the terms of the treaty of the previous year and moved south to dispute Gilbert's authority. An attempt was made at mediation but, as no resolution had been achieved by late 1270, the Welsh prince attacked and destroyed what had been built to date. Gilbert made good the damage the following year, and at the end of 1271 King Henry III himself tried to intercede, appointing two bishops to address the dispute and assuming control of the castle. However, early in 1272 Gilbert's men ejected the mediators and took control of the castle, and building continued.

The speed at which the castle was built is matched only by those built a few years later by Edward I in north-west Wales (see chapter 2). The core of the castle was built from 1268 to about 1271, seemingly in three phases; additions were made by Earl Gilbert in another two phases from about 1277 to the 1290s, and were probably continued under Gilbert's son, Gilbert III (d.1314). However, the details of the precise phasing are still open to academic argument.

The final medieval phase was concerned with major alterations to the castle's hall in the 1320s. In the first period, the central island on which the inner ward sits was created by digging ditches, with water defences retained by embankments to the south and north, as well as islands to the west and east. The eastern island formed the buttressed south dam, with a gatehouse linked to the town at the southern end, and a watermill was built here. The castle that sits on the central island

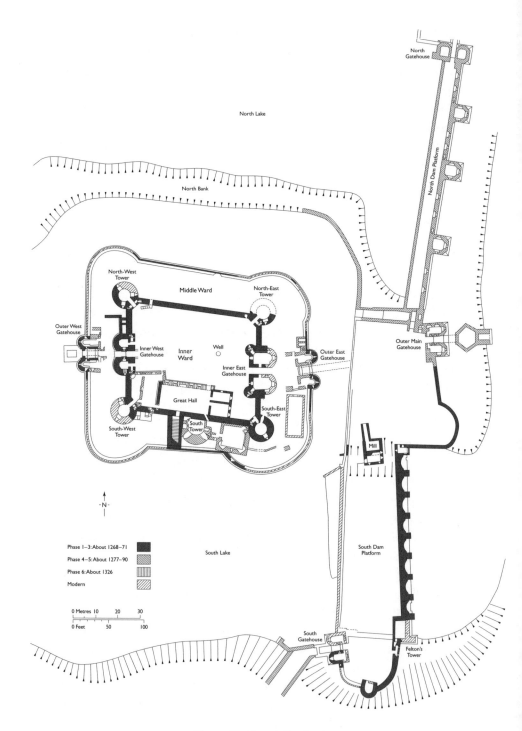

Figure 11: Caerphilly Castle

is concentric. The thin outer curtain (much rebuilt in modern times) is furnished with two small twin-towered gatehouses which stand opposite one another on the east and west sides. At the centre of each of the other two sides is a postern. The rectangular inner ward has two larger twin-towered gatehouses, the east one being similar to that built by Gilbert's father at the Clare castle of Tonbridge in Kent, and large mural circular towers at the four corners. The private apartments, hall, chapel and service rooms lay on the south side of the ward, and linking the hall to the south postern was a covered passage with rooms above.

In the second phase, around 1277 onwards, the south dam's masonry defences were extended northwards. The new dam platform has three spur-buttressed towers, with a gatehouse at the northern end, whilst at the southern end a new outer gatehouse was built. On the central island, the rear of each of the towers of the two small outer gatehouses was enclosed in masonry, whilst on the south-east side of the middle ward a massive D-shaped tower was constructed, possibly for private accommodation as first built.

The whole of the front of the hall, overlooking the inner ward, was rebuilt by Hugh Despenser the younger (d.1326) in work of the highest quality, and the range was reroofed. The large square kitchen tower, on the south side, just to the west of the south-east (leaning) tower, may also be Despenser work of the 1320s. These works marked the last medieval phase, for from the middle of the fourteenth century Caerphilly's history appears to have been one of general abandonment, virtually a white elephant in a conquered Wales. The castle's destruction is something of a mystery. Although a small civil war fort was built in the 1640s immediately across the water to the north-west of the west island, this may not have been constructed as a siege work but, rather, raised by royalist troops to cover the main east–west route. The damage to the castle's towers may not have been civil war slighting, but more a case of the locals raiding the castle for its stone, although gunpowder could have been used in this activity, hence the famous leaning south-east tower.

The third marquess of Bute reroofed the hall in the 1870s, but it was his son, the fourth marquess, who undertook to conserve and rebuild with great care much of the fabric of the castle in the depression years from 1928 until the outbreak of the Second World War. Much of the northern tower of the south dam's gatehouse to the town was rebuilt (a course of tile divides the medieval fabric from that of the twentieth century), as well as the outer wall of Felton's Tower opposite it, at the end of the buttressed dam wall. The front of the east inner gatehouse was also rebuilt, as were much of the west towers of the inner ward. After the Second World War, the restoration and conservation continued with the monument in state care, work which saw the lakes reflooded and hall restored. Recent work by Cadw in the inner ward has seen the opening of the east gatehouse to the public, and also the Braose gallery passage running along the south wall, behind the hall.

Caerphilly was involved in two important events in south Wales at the beginning of the fourteenth century. The first was the ultimately unsuccessful revolt of Llywelyn Bren in the opening months of 1316, local discontent breaking out against those who were running the Clare estates whilst they were under royal control. The town was badly damaged, but the castle held out, although one of the gates and a drawbridge were destroyed. Llywelyn was later to be hanged by Hugh Despenser the younger. The other event was the siege of 1326–7, when the castle was held by 130 men, mainly Welsh, for King Edward II (1307–27). Edward and his favourite Hugh Despenser had fled west from the castle shortly beforehand. A full inventory of what the castle contained was made after the surrender in March 1327. In addition to the names of the garrison, it detailed the weaponry and supplies, 600 silver vessels and coinage to the value of £14,000, not forgetting the personal possessions that the king had abandoned.

One enters the castle across the moat over two modern bridges and a central platform. This platform originally had a drawbridge, and once that had been crossed there could be no further progress until the drawbridge of the main outer gatehouse had been lowered. Running to the north and south of the gatehouse are the formidable walls of the dam, and it will be seen that the three towers on the north have pulled away from the main wall due to subsidence. It is also clear that the lower part of the dam wall was built before the towers, as the masonry of the latter is not bonded into the wall. Spurred buttresses, which tend to date to the late thirteenth century, are prominent features of the towers, the north gatehouse at the end of the dam and the outer gate.

The outer gatehouse, possibly the constable's residence, has survived the centuries well, and this may be due to its use as a prison, certainly in the sixteenth century, although some restoration has been undertaken. The part-level, part-sloping sockets in the sides of the gate-passage are where the axle of the drawbridge would have been received. The passage would have been defended by a portcullis, murder holes, guard chambers and arrowslits. Beyond the passage a staircase leads up to the main floor of the gate. A doorway off a small room at this level led out to the north dam wall (originally there was a small drawbridge at this point), whilst another chamber housed a small kitchen. From the roof of the tower it can seen that the north dam wall-walk had a pit by each tower, to trap the unwary attacker; normally these would have been covered by planking. There was a third drawbridge, with a portcullis, which covered the sluice channel below and gave access to the platform behind the dam wall.

The south dam platform contains the remains of a rare survival, a medieval watermill for milling corn. Adjacent to it, in the dam wall, is the small rectangular tower for the garrison watch, liberally provided with latrines, as is evident from the outfall chutes on the outside. At the southern end of the dam, before the wall curves round to a D-shaped tower and the south gatehouse, there is the much rebuilt Felton's Tower, a structure that controlled the sluices for the waters at this point. Also to be seen on the platform are a number of modern but working replicas of siege engines.

Moving across the moat and through the small outer east gatehouse, one enters the middle ward of the central island. In front is the great inner east gatehouse, to the right the remains of the north-east tower, whilst to the left is the leaning south-east tower, by which is a rectangular storehouse. The leaning tower still has its original openings, on which many of the later reconstructions have been based. Features in the inner curtain wall at this point show that the original wall-walk was covered over to form a passage, the Braose Gallery, and this is even clearer on either side of the south-west tower. The wall that blocks the visitor from continuing west along the middle ward is part of the massive square kitchen tower, beyond which lie the remains of the D-shaped south tower that was used as part of the kitchen and brewhouse complex.

Returning to the east gatehouse of the inner ward, it is noticeable that the front face of the building has been rebuilt (1931–3), as have the battlements. It is not usually open to the public, but the recent reflooring of the second floor of this gatehouse has resulted in public access. The passage had the usual defences of two sets of doors, each with a portcullis, and murder holes. Passage doorways opened into the ground-floor chambers, at the back of both of which was a doorway to a stair turret to the upper floors. The wall-walk on either side of the gatehouse was reached via the first-floor chambers, although for the security of the gate a portcullis guarded each doorway. On the second floor was the hall, with a great fireplace and, as can be seen from the inner ward, it had two very fine, albeit restored, windows. The whole complex was clearly designed to house important guests in well-appointed and secure accommodation, comparable to Marten's Tower at Chepstow (p. 115).

On the left as you enter the inner ward is a range of buildings that contained the hall in the centre, service rooms to the left with the chapel above and private apartments to the right. The hall as we see it today belongs to the 1320s, although it was reroofed in the nineteenth century. One would have entered either the hall to the right or the services rooms (buttery and pantry) to the left. A doorway in the middle of the outer wall of the hall led down to a postern, giving access from the south lake, whilst at the far, dais, end of the hall a doorway opened into the private apartments. Hidden from view, the Braose Gallery mentioned above runs along the top of the outer wall of the hall.

The hall is well lit and has a handsome fireplace. The modern roof timbers rest on 1320s corbels, which are decorated with a series of carved heads.

Most of the south-west tower of the inner ward was restored in the 1930s. The north-west corner tower retains much of its medieval fabric. The entrance to the tower leads to a small lobby, to the right of which is a passage to a latrine; in the centre is the door to the ground-floor chamber or storeroom, and, to the left, a newel staircase rises to the two upper chambers, both with fireplaces. At first-floor level there is access to the wall-walk on the north side of the inner ward, now covered by a modern hourd.

The inner west gatehouse has a number of differences when compared to its east equivalent. It is smaller, the chambers were reached by doorways in the rear walls, and the guard chambers were stone vaulted. However, like the east gatehouse, the doorways through which the wall-walk would be reached were protected by portcullises. The outer west gate gave access to the large island platform beyond, and may have been built round an existing timber framework housing a drawbridge. It has even been suggested that originally the main access to the castle lay on this side, to be reversed in Gilbert de Clare's second construction phase.

The island platform is revetted in masonry, but it is uncertain whether the walls were ever built higher; there may have been just a timber palisade enclosing the interior of the platform known in Welsh as *Y Weringaer*, the people's fort, a name that has led to the suggestion that the purpose of the island was to provide shelter for the townspeople in times of trouble.

Caerwent motte, Monmouthshire

Ordnance Survey: Landranger 171. *ST: 471 904.*
Guidebook. Cadw.

The visitor comes to Caerwent for the Roman town, its temple and town defences. However, in the south-east corner of the Roman walls is a Norman motte, recently conserved by Cadw. The motte sits astride the masonry, and it is presumed that the south-east section of the town within the walls was cut off by a bank and ditch to form a bailey.

Caldicot Castle, Monmouthshire

Ordnance Survey: Landranger 171. *ST: 487 885.*
Entry charge. Guidebook. Local authority.

Caldicot must rank as one of the major castles of south Wales that has not been the subject of a thorough modern architectural and historical analysis. It is a castle that would repay such a study, as there is much of interest. Documentary evidence does exist, especially for the fourteenth century (the first certain reference is for the year 1216), but there has not always been agreement on the exact phasing of the buildings that belong to that century. We know more about the restoration work, particularly on the gatehouse, by J. R. Cobb in the nineteenth century. Cobb also undertook work on the castles of Manorbier (p. 86) and Pembroke (p. 90) in Pembrokeshire.

The castle is often viewed as a traditional motte and bailey. Indeed, the most conspicuous part of the castle, the round keep, stands on a motte in the manner of Bronllys in Breconshire (p. 98).

However, the keep's basement goes deep into the body of the 'motte', and in order for construction to have taken place the original mound, if there had been one, must have been all but removed and 'rebuilt' after the construction of the great round tower in the early thirteenth century.

The early phases of the masonry castle are the work of the Bohun family, Henry (d.1220) and Humphrey (d.1275). So, to the thirteenth century we can assign the keep, the curtain wall, the south-east and south-west towers and the Bohun gateway immediately south of the keep, although there is more than one phase, as the curtain wall and the keep abut one another, rather than being bonded. The gatehouse through which the castle is entered today was built in the first half of the fourteenth century by the ninth Humphrey de Bohun (1337–61), although previously it has been assigned to Thomas Woodstock based on the interpretation of the documentary evidence. The arches in the gate passage are very similar to those in parts of Berkeley Castle, not far away in Gloucestershire, that can be dated to the first half of the fourteenth century. The Woodstock Tower, a small gate or postern tower, was added in the late fourteenth century by Thomas of Woodstock, son of King Edward III, who had married into the Bohun family (a stone in the gateway bears the name 'Thomas').

The gatehouse, restored by Cobb, especially the rear wall and the first-floor hall, is rectangular, with a battered base. The windows belie the defensive nature of the gatehouse. Although the battlements have been restored, original work can be seen at the top of the west tower, with a corbel table on a row of heads. Square towers flank the entrance passage, which had a portcullis and murder holes, and there are doorways into lodges as well as seat recesses in the passage walls. Looking back at the gatehouse from within the bailey, note Cobb's half-timbered and brick building.

The keep is a handsome structure, of fine sandstone ashlar. There are two main floors above a basement chamber or prison. The keep was equipped with a well and latrines. The main chamber lay on the topmost floor; a comfortable apartment, it was well lit, had a fireplace, and a door led to a projecting wooden pent-roofed latrine. The door and the stone supports or corbels for this latrine are clearly visible on the outside.

Cobb restored much of the keep, but the upper part of the tower still has evidence for a heightening which may have been undertaken soon after it had been built. The curtain wall, although later and built in more than one phase, may also date to the first half of the thirteenth century, as the arrowslits match those at Chepstow of the later Marshal period (1230s/1240s).

The gate tower to the south of the keep may have been the original entrance in the early thirteenth century, but is unusual in that its gateway lies in the flank (cf. the Horseshoe Tower at Pembroke (p. 91)) with a postern (?) set into the floor of the gate passage. The entrance was also covered by murder holes.

A circular tower lies at the south-west corner, but is not bonded with the curtain (it may be contemporary with the keep). The curtain then runs up to the later gatehouse. The northern curtain is also early thirteenth century, although the short east stretch has been rebuilt in the later Middle Ages and more recently. At the south-east corner lies a large D-shaped tower, almost comparable to native Welsh towers such as those at Castell y Bere and Ewloe (pp. 19, 45). This may have been a private chamber, or solar tower – or at least converted to one from a defensive tower – possibly associated with a thirteenth-century hall that was replaced in the fourteenth century on the same site. Of the three small windows, with seats, one is above an arrowslit, and the tracery of the east window suggests that the conversion of this tower into a fine residence took place in the later thirteenth century. Also associated with this later work is the fine chimneypiece. Traces of painted wall plaster survive, with false masonry joints in red, a feature also much in evidence at Chepstow (p. 115).

The wall between the south-east tower and the gatehouse is of two builds, the lowest courses being associated with the south-east tower, whilst the upper section is fourteenth century, but seemingly earlier than the gatehouse.

The Woodstock Tower, built in the late 1380s, provided three floors of fine chambers over an entrance passage, the floors all having latrines and fireplaces, as well as windows. The battlements have prominent machicolations.

Traces of internal buildings within the bailey can be seen against the north curtain, which also has two flights of steps to the wall-walk.

Cardiff Castle, Glamorgan

Ordnance Survey: Landranger 171. *ST: 181 766.*
Entry charge. Guidebook. Local authority.

Cardiff Castle (plate 13) has undergone a range of major transformations during its long history – Roman fort, Norman fortress, late medieval and Elizabethan mansion, then the transformations by the Bute family in the late eighteenth and nineteenth centuries and the excavation and great rebuilding of the Roman fort from the 1890s and into the last century.

A considerable amount of the original Roman masonry can still be seen, especially on the south side, near the main entrance, where the late third-century Roman walling of what was the fourth fort on the site lies under a band of pinkish Radyr stone, with the fourth marquess of Bute's reconstruction above. More of the core of the Roman fort can be seen inside.

The Norman castle was probably founded by King William I himself in 1081 when he was in south Wales. For a castle with a long history, or perhaps because of it, there is not a large amount of medieval masonry standing, certainly not standing unaltered. However, the conqueror's castle is represented by the large motte occupying the north-west half of the interior. Cardiff was to become the centre of the lordship of Glamorgan under Robert fitz Hamon from the late eleventh century. The shell keep on the motte was probably built by Robert of Gloucester around 1140. The new entrance to the shell keep and the remains of the masonry wall running from the motte across the interior, originally linking with the Black Tower in the middle of the south side, was built by the Clares in the thirteenth and fourteenth centuries. This new entrance to the shell keep was protected by a formidable structure or forebuilding, clearly visible in eighteenth-century prints and drawings of the castle, but demolished later in that century.

In the early fifteenth century, Richard Beauchamp, earl of Warwick, built a new hall range on the south-west side, and this has remained to form the nucleus of all the later buildings here. The polygonal Beauchamp Tower is a prominent feature of his work. Further improvements were made by the earl of Pembroke, Henry Herbert, in the late sixteenth century, but little remains of these extensive alterations, apart from the windows in the shell keep and the Black Tower.

The west apartments and south side of the castle then underwent a series of major transformations from the late eighteenth century, but particularly in the nineteenth century by the third marquess of Bute, to give the castle the appearance that it has made it so famous today for lovers of things Victorian, but not dwelt on here.

Approaching the entrance to the castle on the south, the restored Black Tower on the left was certainly standing well before 1316, when new lead was applied to its roof. The purpose of the tower was to protect the surprisingly simple gateway to the castle, but by the sixteenth century its main role was as a prison. There are three floors over a vaulted basement, and hard against the west side of the tower is a small annexe that housed latrines originally.

The motte and its shell keep dominate the interior, the keep itself being of one the best examples of its type in Britain. Much of the earth rampart that runs along the north-east and east side of the castle belongs to the initial Norman work of 1081. The Norman polygonal keep was rebuilt on the south-east side about 1300 when a new hall range was added to the interior, and the polygonal gate tower also dates to this later phase. This gate tower has three small chambers over the entrance passage; a doorway off the passage leads out to the edge of the motte. A flight of steps at the rear of the tower lead to the first floor, the steps obscuring an original Norman flight up to the shell keep's wall-walk. Access to the second floor would originally have been only from the hall, the only part of which that survives is the south gable set into the Norman shell keep.

Castell Coch, Glamorgan

Ordnance Survey: Landranger 171. *ST: 131 826.*
Entry charge. Guidebook. Cadw.

Like Cardiff, above, this castle's claim to fame today is the work undertaken in the nineteenth century (1875–91) by the third marquess of Bute and his talented architect, William Burges. However, much remains of the medieval castle, and its very plan dictated Burges's work.

Very little is known about the medieval castle; its only mention in the records is in 1307. It is assumed that the thirteenth-century stronghold of Gilbert de Clare, lord of Glamorgan and the builder of

Caerphilly, was built on the site of a Norman motte, raised to control the route north from Cardiff, at the southern end of the Taff gorge. There is a possibility that there was some masonry here earlier in the thirteenth century, but the massive spur buttresses suggest a date of around 1290 for much of the construction of the castle, after the Edwardian conquest of north Wales. If this dating is correct, it may be that Castell Coch was built more for pleasure than defence, a hunting lodge rather than a fortress.

The motte was clad in masonry with the curtain, perhaps part of an earlier shell keep, built on the northern and western sides, the hall, three towers and a gatehouse occupying the rest of the perimeter. The lower parts of the towers are medieval, with vaulted basements, but the north-east and south-west towers (Well and Kitchen Towers) have more medieval masonry than the south-east or Keep Tower. The lower hall, where the shop is, is also medieval.

The work by William Burges, which was continued after his death in 1881, transformed the castle into the form that has come down to us today. For a full understanding of this, see the current Cadw guidebook.

Castell Dinas (Bwlchyddinas), Breconshire

Ordnance Survey: Landranger 161. *SO: 179 301.* Open access.

A hilltop castle for the very fit! The remains of this stronghold (plate 14) sit within an Iron Age hillfort with multiple defences and, although what is left of the castle is extremely fragmentary (but much must remain below the turf), the archaeology of the site and the surrounding views make the effort to climb up to the castle worthwhile.

Probably founded in the twelfth century, a survey of the castle in 1337 exudes an air of neglect. The outer gate was 'weak and ruinous', although repairs were costed at only £5 in the money of the day! The estimated total cost of the recommended repairs came to £65, but it is unlikely that anything was done as a result. Traces remain of the inner gate at the north end of the site, as well as a square tower close to it, and there is also evidence for other towers.

At the heart of the castle is the rectangular 'enclosure' which marks the site of the rectangular keep or main tower and its surrounding curtain wall. The 1337 survey mentions the 'Great Tower' whose roof and chimneys were in need of repair.

Chepstow Castle, Monmouthshire

Ordnance Survey: Landranger 162. *ST: 533 941.*
Entry charge. Guidebook. Cadw.

Superbly positioned above the river Wye (plate 15; figure 12), this is one of the great strongholds of Europe, and one of the most thoroughly studied castles in recent years.

The castle was founded by William fitz Osbern (d.1071) according to Domesday Book, and the earliest phase of the Great Tower has traditionally been assigned to him. Although there is no doubt that fitz Osbern had a castle here, recent research has now attributed the Great Tower to the Crown, probably William I, who may have commissioned the building on his visit to south Wales in 1081.

To the west of the Great Tower, and only visible from the exterior, is a section of curtain wall associated with the tower, but otherwise little else is known about the structure of the castle until the later twelfth century. Chepstow remained in the possession of the Crown until the early twelfth century, and then it was acquired by the Clare family. In 1189 it passed to William Marshal (d.1219), upon his marriage to the daughter and heiress of Richard de Clare (Strongbow), and it is to his time that the main defences date: the outer gatehouse (its doors dated by tree-ring analysis to the late twelfth century), the towers and gateway of the middle ward, and the curtain and what is currently known as the Marshal's Tower to the west of the Great Tower. Marshal's sons (1219–45), who all died young, continued the work of their father, notably with the strong upper barbican at the extreme west end of the castle, with its gatehouse and well-looped south-west tower. The Marshal sons also heightened the west end of the Great Tower for extra accommodation, whilst the main floor had new windows and was divided by two arches, of which enough masonry remains to show that the quality of this new build was on a par with anything that was to be found in a royal palace or great abbey.

The Bigod family acquired Chepstow through the marriage of Hugh, third earl of Norfolk, to a daughter of William Marshal. The domestic arrangements of the castle were transformed in the later thirteenth century by Roger Bigod, fifth earl of Norfolk (d.1306), at a time when several of his peers were undertaking similar work at their castles, such as Valence at Goodrich and Kidwelly and Clare at

Caerphilly. He may also have been responsible for enclosing the town with a stone wall and mural towers, much of which still stand.

On the north side of the lower bailey, overlooking the river, a new range was constructed, which included a kitchen and a hall, set at differing levels and separated by a passage, buttery and pantry, with private apartments (the earl's chamber) above the service area. A cellar lay beneath. The hall was entered by crossing a drawbridge and entering a porch decorated with heraldic wall-paintings. Following the visit of King Edward I and Queen Eleanor in December 1284, work began on what is now known as Marten's Tower, but is referred to in the accounts as the 'New Tower'. The building was completed around 1293. The purpose of the tower seems to have been to provide fine accommodation for the earl's guests, and perhaps Bigod was hoping for a repeat visit from his monarch. Roger Bigod's later programme of works included the extension of the upper storey of the great tower, continuing the work of the Marshals. Turrets were provided at the corners in which springalds (giant crossbows), ordered in 1298–9, were housed.

As far as the fabric was concerned, little was then done until the sixteenth century when the castle came into the hands of the Somerset earls of Worcester (see also Raglan, p. 134). Charles, first earl (d.1526) and an important figure in the court of Henry VIII, created new timber-framed ranges on both sides of the middle bailey curtain wall and modified other buildings in the lower bailey. New windows are evident in the outer gatehouse and Marten's Tower.

In the English civil war Chepstow was held for the king, but was finally besieged and captured in October 1645. In the second war of 1648 the castle was again held for the king. Just as it was about to be stormed, following a major bombardment, the garrison, having dismissed an earlier call for its surrender, finally capitulated, although no mercy was shown to the royalist commander, Sir Nicholas Kemeys, and he was shot.

After the Restoration of 1660, £500 was spent on the castle to adapt its walls and towers for use by artillery and musketeers. Chepstow also housed the regicide Henry Marten (d.1680) in the tower that now bears his name. Inventories of 1672 and 1679 list a range of munitions held in the castle, including cannon. In 1685 the garrison was stood down, parts of the castle were demolished and fixtures and fittings were removed.

Nail and glass manufactories were set up in the lower bailey in the eighteenth century, and other buildings were to be found there, such as a stable. With the increasing popularity of the Wye tour after the publication of William Gilpin's account of his tour in 1770, which first appeared in print dated 1782, visitors coming to the castle grew in number, and at this time Marten's Tower was still roofed and floored. The industrial buildings were removed in the nineteenth century by the eighth duke of Beaufort (d.1899), and some conservation of the ruins was undertaken. This was continued by the Lysaght family who acquired the castle in 1905.

The main entrance, at the east end of the ridge on which the castle stands, is guarded by a twin-towered gatehouse, one of the earliest of its kind in Europe. It retains many of its arrowslits, but the windows are additions made in the sixteenth century, whilst the battlements date to the later seventeenth century, a time when most of the castle's battlements were altered to take cannon and muskets. The stub of masonry on one of the towers is all that remains of a small barbican. The entrance passage into the lower bailey had strong doors (displayed inside the castle) and two portcullises. The gatehouse has three floors, and additional chambers were built behind it in the late thirteenth century. The ground floor of the tower nearest the river was a prison, while the tower on the other side housed the guard chamber.

The other imposing feature at this end of the castle is Marten's Tower, with its spur buttresses, figured battlements and the square chapel on its northern side. It probably stands on the site of a mural tower of the Marshal period. It consists of three main floors above a basement, and there was even a room at attic level. The windows overlooking the lower bailey are sixteenth-century additions. This great tower could be isolated from the rest of the castle by doorways and portcullises at ground and wall-walk levels. The interior walls were plastered and painted, and some of this scheme remains to be seen today. The small chapel lies off the staircase to the roof level, and traces of its lead roof are still visible. It has two side narrow windows, each with a seat, and the main, east, window still preserves its carved rosette decoration. The rectangular slot in the floor would have housed the portcullis that protected the doorway to the wall-walk on the floor below. When raised, the portcullis would have intruded into the room – a not uncommon arrangement in castle chapels.

The rest of the lower bailey is dominated by the extensive Bigod range that runs along the north side, overlooking the river. Behind the gatehouse is the kitchen and its larder, with rooms above it, where the shop now is. The kitchen was open to the roof and lit by a handsome window overlooking the courtyard, and originally two on the other side. The large arch in the end wall originally had three serving hatches, through which food would be passed to be taken up to the hall. Beyond the kitchen is a passage that leads to a double-seater latrine chamber and to steps down to the fine vaulted cellar, into which goods could be winched up from boats on the river. Also off the passage, opposite the kitchen, is a door into an administrative office, whilst beyond it is the doorway to the stairs up to the hall.

The main entrance to the hall was through the porch, entered by crossing a small bridge. Two painted shields can be seen inside the porch, above the door that led to the hall. At one end of the hall are three doorways, the central one opening on to the stairs mentioned above, the others leading into originally the buttery (left) and pantry (right). In the same wall is a blocked window, and to the left the doorway to the earl of Norfolk's private accommodation, the 'Gloriette', which would have been reached by wooden steps. At the opposite end of the hall was the dais where the lord would have sat.

Much of the curtain wall on the opposite side of the lower bailey dates to the later seventeenth century onwards, the large arched

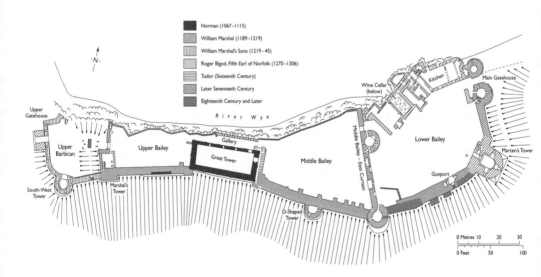

Figure 12: Chepstow Castle

opening being a gunport. However, the wall and two towers that mark the division of the lower and middle baileys date to the William Marshal period, including the two towers; the larger tower controls the gateway into the middle bailey. The wooden doors here date to the sixteenth century. The curtain walls and the towers were altered in the early sixteenth century, when fireplaces and other features were added as part of a new range built by the first earl of Worcester on either side of the earlier curtain.

The thin riverside wall of the middle bailey is modern. The defences on the opposite side were thickened in the late seventeenth century, but the D-shaped tower and much of the outer face of the curtain wall belong to the Marshal period. Standing between the middle and upper baileys is the Norman great tower. When first built, the tower consisted of a basement with the main floor above. The main entrance was through the east doorway, with a carved semi-circular panel above, and then on up a mural staircase to the first floor. Running round the tower with its shallow buttresses is a band of reused Roman tile, probably from Caerwent (p. 107).The entrance used today, into the basement, leading off from the gallery built in the late thirteenth century, is also Norman.

Standing within the tower, in the basement storeroom, one can see the main features that survive from the original Norman build – a series of niches, once more extensive, with traces of the original decorative plasterwork, a remarkable survival. The purpose of these niches is not known, but perhaps leading magnates, even the king, sat here on certain major occasions. Handsome new windows were added in the early thirteenth century, and at the same time another floor was added at the west end. The main floor was divided by a double arch, long since destroyed, although where this addition met the walls of the tower enough remains to show that this carved masonry was of the highest quality. The final phase in the tower's building history was when the second floor was extended eastwards across it in the late thirteenth century.

The thin riverside wall of the upper bailey is early modern, while opposite we have again a later seventeenth-century thickening of the Marshal-period curtain. The main feature of this part of the castle is the Marshal's Tower and, although much ruined, enough survives to show that this tower housed a comfortable first-floor chamber over its own kitchen. One of the windows was partly blocked to form a musket loop in the late seventeenth century. The tower may well have been the private chamber of William Marshal himself and his wife in the early 1200s.

The final part of the castle is the barbican at the west end of the castle. This is one of the most formidable barbicans of a castle in Wales. It was built during the time of one or more of William Marshal's sons (1219–45). The wall butts against the Marshal's Tower and runs westward and then north to the cliff edge, ending in a latrine turret. A postern, now blocked, is in the ditch that divides the barbican from the Marshal's Tower and the entrance to the upper bailey. The south-west tower, built as open backed, had a purely military function, with three floors each containing four arrowslits, set over an unlit basement; a newel stair linked the floors and gave access to the wall-walk. A stub of walling on the outside of the tower may have linked the castle with the Port Wall, the town's defences that can be seen across the Dell by a car park and beyond. The original entrance to the barbican was a simple gateway, but it was extended in the later thirteenth century to form a gate tower with drawbridge and portcullis, as well as murder holes. The barbican entrance also led out to the gardens associated with the castle on this side. The arrowlooped wall between the gate tower and the south-west tower has a parapet and a parados – in other words, battlements shielding the wall-walk on both sides. This not only made the wall-walk safer, but it also gave archers the ability to shoot from the protection of the parados into the interior of the barbican should a hostile force break through the entrance.

Coity Castle, Glamorgan

Ordnance Survey: Landranger 170. *SS: 923 816*.
Guidebook. Cadw.

Like its neighbouring castles of Bridgend (Newcastle) and Ogmore (pp. 97, 129), this castle began as an earth-and-timber ringwork, possibly replacing the 'Oldcastle' that existed in Bridgend (but see also Bridgend, above). It was one of the few castles in Glamorgan to remain in the same family, the Turbervilles, for several generations.

The timber palisade of the ringwork was replaced with a stone curtain wall in the late twelfth century, possibly by the second Payn de

Turberville (d.1207). At the same time Payn built a small rectangular keep next to the entrance to the inner ward, thus placing the keep in an offensive position comparable to that at Ogmore (p. 129) and other castles in south Wales. The work at Coity must have been deemed sufficient for the Turbervilles' needs in the thirteenth century, for nothing else was done at the castle until the fourteenth century, unless the large, undated, rectangular building in the inner ward is pre-1300.

In the fourteenth century the castle was converted into a comfortable fortified mansion, with the emphasis on improved accommodation, either by the third Payn de Turberville (d.1318) or his son, Gilbert, who held the castle until about 1349. The rectangular outer ward was strengthened with a masonry curtain wall with small rectangular or square towers and a gatehouse. A new gatehouse was built at the entrance to the inner ward, and a rectangular latrine tower was added to the north side of the keep. A rounded tower built out from the inner curtain on the south side served a similar purpose, providing the latrines for a new domestic range containing a hall and accommodation over services such as the kitchen.

During the Owain Glyndŵr revolt, the castle was besieged twice, in 1404 and 1405. Considerable damage was done to the fabric, especially the north wall of the inner ward, leaving much repair work to be undertaken by the Berkerolles and Gamage families who held the castle around this time. This wall was rebuilt and a new gatehouse built next to it. Also in the inner ward, a chapel, planned in the fourteenth century, was finally built. In the outer ward, siege damage was repaired, the outer gate was rebuilt and a new tower was built at the south-west corner. The south tower was converted into a gatehouse and a new wall added running from this south gate to the inner ward. At the same time a large barn was built against the outer ward's south wall, which was strengthened with buttresses at the same time.

The Gamages held the castle until the late sixteenth century, and as at Bridgend (Newcastle) (p. 98), they rebuilt a number of windows in the familiar Tudor style in the upper floor of the keep and the south range. Fireplaces were also added to the upper floors of the lodgings and improvements made to the kitchen. An additional storey was added to the keep and its north annexe. In 1584 the castle passed into the hands of the Sidney family and, although Coity was maintained until the eighteenth century, thereafter it gradually fell into ruin.

Entering through the west gatehouse, the footings are all that remains of the once great barn would have dominated the outer ward. Approaching the inner ward there is a tower to the left, with the south gatehouse to the right. Originally, the two wards would have been separated by a ditch, but this has long since been infilled, probably in the sixteenth century. Running from the south gate to the curtain wall of the inner ward is a length of fifteenth-century wall, ending with a latrine turret. The wall is pierced by a series of loops, probably designed for guns. Note that above the loops the original battlements have been blocked, and at the same time the wall was heightened.

Arrowslits and gunloops

Arrowslits or loops begin to appear in castle towers and gatehouses in Britain from the late twelfth century. They enabled archers to cover the ground in front of their position, as well as flank a castle's defences on either side. Some of the best early examples can be seen at Chepstow (p. 113); these date to the time of William Marshal and his sons, 1189–1245. Loops can vary from castle to castle. The simplest form is a vertical slit, sometimes ending in a small round or square hole called an oillet. Others have cross-slits to improve an archer's field of view. An interesting variant can be seen at White Castle where the cross-slits are staggered; archers who have experimented behind such loops have said that the staggered form improves the field of vision. At Caernarfon Castle (p. 16), the north curtain has a number of ingeniously constricted slits, each one of which could be manned by at least three archers, as internally there are three embrasures to each loop.

Arrowslits enabled a castle's garrison to shoot from relative safety, although a skilful archer outside could place his arrow or crossbow bolt through the narrow opening. Men-at-arms would also be stationed on the battlements in the event of an attack, and the solid part of battlements (merlons) could also have arrowslits. Archers with either longbows or crossbows would have used arrowslits, although a crossbow would have been easier to use if the archer was actually positioned within an embrasure and space was restricted.

Early gunloops were either of the inverted keyhole type, with a large circular opening at the base of a slit, or just a plain circular hole. Gunloops start appearing in England in the late fourteenth century, but those in Wales date to the following century. The best examples in Wales can be seen at Raglan Castle (p. 135).

The inner gatehouse was grafted on to the side of the keep on one side, with a rectangular guard chamber on the other; the passage originally had doors and a portcullis, as well as a doorway into the chamber, from which a mural stair led to the upper levels. The keep originally had two floors over a basement, with a first-floor entrance, but a ground-floor doorway was inserted in the fourteenth century; at the same time a central pillar was added to support new vaulted upper floors.

Around the south side, running from the inner gatehouse, is the service range, divided by a cross-wall with fireplaces and ovens in the sixteenth century. There is also a malting kiln in one corner. Above this range was the accommodation for the household. Beyond, there is a once vaulted undercroft, over which stood the hall. It was reached by a grand staircase on the far side, beyond which lay the later chapel. The latrine tower, which could be reached from both the hall and the undercroft, had latrines on the first and second floors and a chamber on the uppermost.

The modest north-east gatehouse is the best surviving feature of the castle. With a central passage, originally vaulted and with a drawbridge, portcullis and doorway, there was a small porter's room overlooking the inner ward, but this is now blocked. A newel staircase led up to the first floor, and so to the top floor, which was well appointed, with fireplace, latrine and several windows. The gatehouse also had access to the wall-walk on either side.

Crickhowell Castle, Breconshire

Ordnance Survey: Landranger 161. *SO: 218 182.* **Local authority.**

The castle belonged to the Turberville family in the twelfth century, passing by marriage to Sir Grimbald Pauncefote in the late thirteenth century. The Mortimers held Crickhowell in the fourteenth century, but it was returned to the Pauncefotes in 1402, it time for it to be severely damaged by the forces of Owain Glyndŵr.

This stronghold, also know as Alisby's Castle, consists of a tall motte, with the remains of a shell keep, below which are the fragments of a thirteenth-century gatehouse that connected the bailey to the motte. Part of one of the gatehouse towers survives to some height, while the other has been reduced to its foundations.

The part of the castle that is most obvious when viewed from the main road is the late thirteenth-century pair of conjoined towers, on the south-east side of the bailey. One is rectangular, the other rounded, and this arrangement is comparable to similar constructions at Abergavenny Castle (p. 96) and also at Brecon. Only part of the rectangular tower still stands, although it can seen with its walls complete in late nineteenth-century photographs. The towers would have provided well-appointed accommodation in the castle from the later thirteenth century.

Looking north into the town from the top of the motte one can see what looks like a medieval round tower, but this is more likely to be a later feature, a folly, constructed from parts of the castle's masonry.

Grosmont Castle, Monmouthshire

See **The Three Castles**

Kenfig Castle, Glamorgan

Ordnance Survey: Landranger 170. *SS: 801 826.*
Nature reserve; footpath.

Much of the castle and the medieval town associated with it now lie buried by the dunes and flora of the nature reserve of Kenfig Burrows. All that survives of the castle is the stump of masonry that is the keep, with traces of the curtain wall and a gatehouse. Most of the remains were uncovered in the course of excavations in the first half of the twentieth century. The castle and town were attacked and burnt by the Welsh on several occasions in the later twelfth and thirteenth and early fourteenth centuries.

The first castle was probably a ringwork, in the middle of which a keep was added some time in the twelfth century while a timber palisade still enclosed the castle. In the thirteenth century a latrine turret was added on the north side of the keep and, some time later, towards the end of that century, the palisade was replaced by a stone wall with a gatehouse and the south side of the keep was rebuilt. It was in this latter phase that the interior of the castle was raised, burying much of the keep up to the level of its first floor, although a new basement doorway was added at the same time.

By the fifteenth century, Kenfig was disappearing under the relentless approach of the sand, the site being abandoned for the higher ground at nearby Pyle and Mawdlam.

Llanblethian Castle

See **St Quentin's Castle**

Llandaff, Bishop's Palace, Cardiff, Glamorgan

Ordnance Survey: Landranger 170. *ST: 156 780.* Local authority.

This castle or fortified bishop's palace was probably the work of William de Braose, bishop of Llandaff (1266–87). It remained the residence of subsequent bishops until the later fifteenth century, when the palace at Mathern in Monmouthshire became the main residence and that at Llandaff passed into the hands of the Mathew family. By the late eighteenth century much of the place was in ruins, but engravings of the period show an inn built against the outside of the gatehouse, which was still thatched, although in a poor state.

The gatehouse and the west side of the castle, with the square south-west tower, are the best surviving parts of the castle. There is a small circular tower at the south-east corner, but very little remains of the hall to the east of the gatehouse. The curtain wall survives on the west and east sides, enclosing the modern garden.

The rectangular, twin-towered gatehouse, the tops of its spur buttresses still visible, is very similar to that built at the end of the north dam at Caerphilly (p. 104). The gate's central passage had a portcullis and one set of doors beyond. At the end of the passage a doorway on the right led into the west tower's ground-floor guard chamber; another doorway just beyond it opened onto the stairs to the upper level. There was a basement below the guard chamber; but this has been filled in. The basement and ground-floor rooms in the east tower of the gatehouse are bleak and would seem to have been prisons. Windows on the west side of the first floor of the gatehouse are sixteenth-century additions.

The rectangular range to the east of the gatehouse had a hall and chamber on the first floor, with a projecting turret that probably housed the bishop's chapel. The round south-east tower had a comfortable chamber on its first floor, with a fireplace and latrine; the room was lit by a window and a loop. The wall that runs between the south-east and south-west towers, dividing the castle from the Cathedral School, is modern.

The south-west tower had two floors above a basement, and could be entered via two mural staircases. A double latrine served the tower on the east side. The curtain wall that runs from the tower to the gatehouse is almost intact, lacking only its battlements. The upper part of the curtain wall butts against the gatehouse, indicating that that wall was raised to its final height only after the gate had been finished.

Loughor Castle, Glamorgan

Ordnance Survey: Landranger 159. *SS: 564 980.*
Guidebook (Gower). Cadw.

Although at first glance the castle looks as though it was originally a motte, archaeological excavations have shown that Loughor was originally a Norman ringwork, built in the early twelfth century. The central area was gradually filled in following various destructions by the Welsh, for example, in 1151 and 1215, to create a level platform. The castle was built in the corner of a Roman fort.

The rectangular tower on the mound was added in the late thirteenth century, and had a single room on both the first and second floors, set over a basement; the upper floors both had a fireplace and a latrine. A doorway in the east wall led into the basement, whilst

Concentric castles

A truly concentric castle has an inner curtain wall enveloped by a lower outer one, best seen in Wales at Beaumaris and Caerphilly (pp. 11, 100), thus providing two lines of defence (figures 2 and 11). A similar arrangement can be seen at Kidwelly (p. 75) (figure 9), but here the side naturally protected by the slope down to the river is defended only by the main curtain wall running along the crest of the slope, with a thin wall, or mantlet, in the centre in front of the hall range.

another doorway at the south-east corner led to a spiral staircase up to the first floor. That corner, complete with staircase, has fallen away from the tower.

When the tower was built, the castle already had a curtain wall encircling the mound, possibly built around 1200.

Monmouth Castle, Monmouthshire

Ordnance Survey: Landranger 162. *SO: 506 129.* Cadw.

Precious little remains of Monmouth Castle, the site of its great thirteenth-century round keep now being occupied by Great Castle House, built by the third marquess of Worcester / first duke of Beaufort about 1673 (now occupied by the Royal Monmouthshire Royal Engineers).

However, what does survive is of interest, namely, the earlier great tower or keep, and the hall. Built in the twelfth century, the keep has pilaster buttresses (as at Chepstow's great tower). Three original windows light the basement, whilst on the floor above a window on the south is of the same date. Like Grosmont, the castle was remodelled by the Lancasters, perhaps by Henry of Grosmont; the main surviving feature of this phase is the two-light east window.

The great hall (or courtroom) is linked obliquely with the keep, and was probably built by Henry III's son Edmund Crouchback, earl of Lancaster, soon after he had acquired the castle in 1267 (along with the Three Castles). It was open to the roof.

Monnow Bridge and Gate, Monmouthshire

Ordnance Survey: Landranger 162. *SO: 504 125.* Local authority.

The bridge and gate at the opposite end of Monmouth to the castle date to the late thirteenth century, possibly replacing the one whose timbers, discovered in 1988, have been dated to the 1170s. It is a rare example of a fortified bridge, and only very recently has it been relieved of vehicular traffic.

The bridge itself is said to date from 1272, with the machicolated gatehouse added a few years later (about 1300), although the uppermost storey and roof are eighteenth century and later. The pedestrian passageways are nineteenth century, inserted when the bridge was widened. The gatehouse has a corbelled latrine on one side, and the entrance passage was defended by a portcullis.

Morlais Castle, Merthyr Tydfil, Glamorgan

Ordnance Survey: Landranger 160. *SO: 048 097.*
Open access via golf course footpath.

The fragmentary remains of this great, albeit seemingly unfinished fortress – its position made more dramatic by the quarrying that has gone on around it – sit at the extreme northern limit of the lordship of Glamorgan, overlooking the Brecon lands of the earldom of Hereford to the north. It was begun around 1288, but work was interrupted for two reasons. First, Humphrey de Bohun, earl of Hereford, complained that the castle encroached on his lands, leading to a major dispute in which King Edward I had to intervene. Secondly, the revolt of Madog ap Llywelyn in north Wales spread to the south, and the local Welsh took a number of castles such as Kenfig (see p. 122) and Morlais. The Welsh in Glamorgan made peace with the king in 1295, and the Crown retained Morlais until shortly before Gilbert de Clare's death in December 1295, but the castle remained abandoned.

Massive rock-cut ditches surround the castle on three sides; quarrying has removed the west ditch and part of that on the north. The humps and bumps that mark the line of the curtain walls and the position of the towers and internal buildings are best appreciated from aerial views of the castle, but the impressive vaulted basement of the great south tower, a building of keep-like proportions, can still be seen. In the nineteenth century, fireplaces and latrines on the upper floor still survived. This tower, at one end of the outer ward, overlooks a platform that lies between it and the ditch, and a short stretch of curtain wall runs west of it to a smaller tower; between the two was a small gateway or postern.

To the north of the south tower, a D-shaped tower projects from the east curtain, and is backed by a range of rectangular buildings. Further north lay the main entrance, overlooked by another D-shaped tower. This entrance marked the end of a cross-wall that divided the inner and outer wards. Close to this wall in the outer ward is the massive rock-cut cistern, dug to provide water.

There are foundations of a number of buildings in the inner ward, but the main feature is the tower that sat at the extreme north end of the castle, also of keep-like proportions. Sadly, little is left of this building, but an engraving of 1741 by the Buck brothers depicts a very substantial building that must have been raised to at least its second storey by the time that work ceased in the 1290s.

Neath Castle, Glamorgan

Ordnance Survey: Landranger 170. *SS: 753 978.* Local authority.

The Normans first built a castle at Neath in the early twelfth century, located near the site of the Roman fort on the west side of the river. That land was soon to be passed to the newly founded abbey and the existing castle, lying on the east side of the river, was probably founded by Robert, earl of Gloucester, around 1140. It was an earth-and-timber ringwork and, although a tower is mentioned in the 1180s, this still may have been of wood. In the hands of the Clare earls of Gloucester, in the thirteenth century, this small castle's ability to withstand a formidable Welsh attack in 1258 would suggest that by this time the castle's timber defences had been replaced by stone, a pattern of development to be seen at numerous other castles in south Wales.

The initial work may have been carried out by Earl Richard in the 1240s, the castle's curtain wall having two D-shaped towers, one with a large latrine turret, and a small gateway or postern. Neath was transformed some time in the early fourteenth century, possibly after the destruction wrought in 1321 by those lords who had rebelled against King Edward II and his favourite Hugh Despenser, lord of Glamorgan.

Neath has a fine twin-towered gatehouse, its outer face still standing to almost its original full height, but the structure is badly truncated within. Utilizing the base of one of the earlier D-shaped towers, it was built over the earlier postern with the second tower on the other side. The postern's original steps were buried, and part of its passage was converted into the new gatehouse's drawbridge pit. The new gate-passage had a portcullis and doors, and there were two murder holes covering the immediate entrance. The gatehouse contains a number of loops and windows. It has been suggested that the stretch of curtain wall running west from the south tower of the gatehouse may be part of Neath's town wall.

A number of fourteenth-century buildings ranged round the interior were discovered through excavation, but the circular depression in the middle dates to more recent times and was a cockpit, seventeenth or eighteenth century in origin.

Newcastle, Bridgend
See **Bridgend**

Newport Castle, Monmouthshire

Ordnance Survey: Landranger 171. *ST: 312 884.* Cadw.

Although Newport Castle, at the time of writing, is closed for the foreseeable future for health and safety reasons, the ability to view it from a bridge in the city (and on the train in and out of the station) makes its inclusion worthwhile.

The castle lies on the river Usk and was built in the fourteenth century (Newport's first castle was nearer St Woolos Cathedral). In plan the castle was quadrangular, but only the east side, overlooking the river, survives, and it is likely that the rest of the castle simply comprised a curtain wall. The castle may have been built by Ralph, earl of Stafford in the later fourteenth century, but considerable refinement of the accommodation was undertaken by Humphrey Stafford, later duke of Buckingham, towards the end of the first half of the fifteenth century. The castle's story from the sixteenth century was one of decline; it became a tannery, then a brewery, in the nineteenth century.

The north and south spur-buttressed towers lie at either end of the curtain wall, with the water gate in the centre. The first-floor hall lay on the north side of the water gate and has windows and a fireplace in the riverside wall. The north tower has two floors over a basement, and excavations to the west of it in the 1970s revealed the site of the north gate as well as a latrine block. To the south of the water gate was the kitchen. The south tower survives better than its northern equivalent, with windows on its three floors, fireplaces and a latrine. This tower clearly accommodated the lords of the castle and it was originally reached via a gallery running between it and the water gate.

Above the entrance passage (with portcullis) of the water gate – an entrance designed for boats – is the presence chamber, a handsome vaulted room that originally extended into the main body of the castle.

There would have been another room above, possibly the chapel. The presence chamber would have been used by the duke of Buckingham for formal ceremonial and estate business occasions.

Ogmore Castle, Glamorgan

Ordnance Survey: Landranger 170. *SS: 882 769.*
Guidebook. Cadw.

The castle was founded about the same time as Coity (p. 118) and the Newcastle at Bridgend (p. 97). The ringwork and bailey were built by William de Londres on the bank of the Ewenny river, probably around 1100. Ogmore always remained simple and unsophisticated in plan, with an early twelfth-century keep and a curtain wall round the ringwork or inner ward built in the early thirteenth century. Thereafter, little was done, apart from some late medieval internal buildings, including a courthouse in the outer ward. The defences of the latter always remained of timber; there is no stone curtain wall here.

The keep is thought to have been built by Maurice de Londres (d.1149), whose tomb, beautifully carved in the thirteenth century, can be seen at nearby Ewenny Priory, which had been founded by his father, William. In addition to the inner ward curtain wall, the thirteenth century saw the construction of a gate tower next to the keep and wing walls across the moat between the inner and outer wards. Other modifications included the addition of an upper storey to the keep and a latrine turret against the keep's north-west corner. It is uncertain who was responsible for these additions, as the Ogmore heiress, Hawise de Londres (d.1274), had three husbands: Walter de Braose, possibly killed in 1233/4; Henry, one of the Coity Turbervilles, who died before 1240; and Patrick de Chaworth, killed by the Welsh in 1258. The castle later became part of the Welsh lands of the Duchy of Lancaster.

The remains of a limekiln can be seen in the outer ward, seemingly built in the late thirteenth century to provide lime for mortar for some work on the castle. The footings of various undated, but late medieval buildings can be seen in the inner ward, but the best surviving structure of this period is the rectangular building in the outer ward, known as the Court House. Under repair in the 1450s, it may have been built in the previous century; it was used to hold court sessions from the fifteenth century through to the early nineteenth century. However, the castle as a whole was considered to be in a poor state, even destroyed, following damage done at the same time as the attacks on Coity in 1404–5.

Entrance to the castle is through the outer ward, with the Court House on the left, built into the remains of the limekiln, as well as the remains of an early thirteenth-century structure. A doorway leads into the Court House, and in the opposing wall is a narrow doorway that led out towards the river.

A modern bridge leads the visitor across the moat, for moat it is, or was, as openings in the wing walls allowed water in to enclose the inner ward at high tide. The gate tower was of simple design; it originally had a drawbridge and doors, but there was no portcullis. The gate passage has an alcove in a side wall, presumably for the porter. The chamber above the gate passage was reached from the keep and along the wall-walk.

The keep would have been entered from an external staircase to the first floor, but another entrance directly into the basement was inserted in the thirteenth century. The first floor was divided into two chambers by a wooden partition, the northern one with the fireplace, the southern lit by two windows. The first-floor fireplace exhibits some of the earliest Norman stone carving in a secular context in Glamorgan. The later second floor has a small fireplace, and a newel stair was added to link the two upper floors as well as give access to the new latrine turret.

Against the river side of the keep is an area which was the site of the kitchen, while overlooking the river is the rectangular hall. Just south of the hall is an enigmatic building, which like the keep is a Norman building, but is possibly late twelfth century. This rectangular 'cellar' may have been used for storage, steps down a vaulted passage leading into the basement. However, it is possible that the cellar was part of a larger building, having an upper storey of wood or stone. In the nineteenth century it was used as a limekiln. Short passages in the curtain wall near the cellar led to latrine turrets.

The wall on the south and east sides of the inner ward has the best surviving section of the curtain. Some of the wall-walk still survives, as do sections of the battlements.

Oystermouth Castle, Glamorgan

Ordnance Survey: Landranger 159. *SS: 613 883.*

Entry charge (interior open Easter to September). Local authority.

Set on a hill overlooking Swansea Bay, two aspects of this castle are immediately noticeable: the strange looking gatehouse (see below) and the fine windows of the best-preserved part of the castle, the fourteenth-century chapel.

William de Londres, who founded Ogmore Castle (p. 129) is thought also to have established the first castle here in the early twelfth century. Although the form of the castle is not known, it is likely to have been a ringwork, in common with so many other castles along the coastal area of south Wales. The castle later became linked with the lords of Gower, and so was in the hands of various families, such as Braose and Mowbray, during the Middle Ages and later, passing to the Somerset earls of Worcester from the sixteenth century onwards, although by this time much of the castle seems to have been in ruins. However, there is evidence of domestic additions to the gatehouse in the sixteenth century.

Apart from the Norman keep, most of the masonry is of various phases of the Braose period, in the thirteenth century, whilst the chapel is assigned to the Mowbray years.

The entrance to the castle is through a mid- to later thirteenth-century twin-towered gatehouse. The demolition of the outer walls of the gatehouse's round towers is what gives the building its rather strange appearance, although the gate passage survives. Unlike the great gatehouses of the late thirteenth century, such as at Caerphilly (p. 103) and Harlech (p. 36), that at Oystermouth was a simpler structure. Its passage had only one set of doors and one portcullis, and there were no doorways off the passage to the guard chambers; the rooms in the gatehouse towers were reached via passages entered from the rear of the building.

Entering the triangular courtyard there is a range of late medieval buildings on each side, built against the curtain wall that is contemporary with the gatehouse. Beyond, to the right, is the chapel; the Norman keep and its later porch are in the middle, and to the left is the thirteenth-century west range, with a kitchen on the first floor and the north-west block beyond.

Only the basement walling of the keep survives to any great extent, for in the early thirteenth century the keep was rebuilt and converted into the main accommodation suite - the addition of a range on its northern side doubled the size of the building. The original north wall of the keep became the spine wall of the new central block and had fireplaces added to it. In common with other Norman keeps, the original main entrance would have been on the first floor. In the thirteenth century, a doorway was inserted at ground level, soon to be replaced by another next to it; the latter was enclosed by a porch at the same time as the chapel was built. When the central block was created, a newel stair was built in the north-west corner of the keep, and encircling the base of this stair is a passage that leads from the block to the north-west area of the castle.

The main accommodation of the central block lay on the first floor. The hall was in the southern half of the range, with a private room or solar on the uppermost floor on the north side. The hall may have been open to the roof. As new buildings were added around the central block, doorways were inserted to improve circulation. Thus one could pass easily from the central building to the north-west range on one side and to the chapel on the south-east side.

The chapel, with its window tracery restored accurately in the nineteenth century, is a fine example of later medieval architecture. It consists of a well-lit first-floor chamber with a fireplace and latrine, over a basement, possibly a kitchen, with the chapel itself on the top floor. The chapel was lit by five handsome windows, and another fine survival is the piscina in the south-east corner. The chapel contains two opposing vaulted and lit recesses in the north and south walls, backing the chimney flues, and it has been suggested that they were confessionals. The southern recess has evidence of painted decoration.

Penlle'r Castell, Glamorgan

Ordnance Survey: Landranger 159. *SN: 665 096.*
Accessible from the road.

Although the castle here is not mentioned until the late sixteenth century, when it was described as an utter ruin, Penlle'r Castell has been identified as the 'new castle in Gower' mentioned in 1252 as being held by the second William de Braose. In that year, it was destroyed by the neighbouring Welsh, although it may have been repaired when restored to Braose. Unlike most castles, its function would have been purely military, to guard and warn against Welsh incursions south into Gower and Swansea.

The castle consists of a massive earthwork surrounded by a deep ditch, and the dumps of spoil on the counterscarp suggest that Braose's castle was attacked whilst still under construction. The platform is divided into two by a ditch which, however, terminates at one end before it reaches the main ditch, leaving a bank connecting the two sections. Both areas contain the remains of a quadrangular building, and other masonry was noted in explorations of the site in the last century.

Pennard Castle, Glamorgan

Ordnance Survey: Landranger 159. *SS: 544 885.* Open access.

On open land overlooking Three Cliffs Bay and Pennard Pill, Gower, the castle is one of the least impressive in south Wales. A Norman ringwork was established here in the twelfth century, and across the Pill from the castle is Penmaen Burrows where another small Norman ringwork was thoroughly excavated in the 1960s. All that remains of the early castle at Pennard is a twelfth-century stone rectangular hall within the later walls. Like Kenfig (p. 122), the castle appears to have been abandoned in the late Middle Ages due to the encroaching sand.

Some time in the late thirteenth or early fourteenth century, the Braose or Mowbray family rebuilt the castle. A twin-towered gatehouse was built on the east side, and a curtain wall was raised around the original ringwork, with a small semicircular tower on the north-west side. Some time later a square building was added by this small tower.

The gatehouse passage had one set of doors and a portcullis, although the latter's grooves did not run down all the way to the ground. The entrances to the chambers were from doorways at the rear of the towers. The upper floor would have been reached by wooden steps. The curtain wall survives best on the north side, running round to the small tower. This tower contains a latrine, and next to it is a buttress supporting another latrine.

The square tower on the west side of the castle, with views overlooking the Pill, was purely residential, and consisted of a first floor over a basement.

Raglan Castle, Monmouthshire

Ordnance Survey: Landranger 161. *SO: 415 083.*
Entry charge. Guidebook. Cadw.

The castle or fortress-palace of Raglan (plate 16; figure 13) is predominantly a fifteenth-century building with sixteenth- and early seventeenth-century additions, but it has been suggested that the present great tower stands on the site of an earlier castle, perhaps a motte and bailey, positioned to command an important crossroads. The Bloet family held Raglan from the late twelfth century until the heiress married Sir James Berkeley in the late fourteenth century, and there is both archaeological and documentary evidence for a manor house or castle on the site. Thirteenth-century floor tiles were discovered when Raglan was undergoing conservation in the 1940s, and a document of 1375 provides details of repairs carried out to the hall, as well as to the lord's solar and latrine.

In 1406 the Bloet heiress, Elizabeth, took as her second husband William ap Thomas (d.1445), the fifth son of a minor Welsh gentry family. William was later to improve his social and financial status, taking as his second wife Gwladus, the daughter of Sir Dafydd Gam and widow of Sir Roger Vaughan of Tretower (p. 146), two knights who fell at Agincourt. The fine alabaster tomb of William and Gwladus can be seen in St Mary's Church, Abergavenny. In 1432 William purchased Raglan from the Berkeley family, and it is thought that it was from this time that he began to transform the manor house or castle of the Bloets into the great building that we see today.

Although it has been argued that the great tower was built by Sir William Herbert, ap Thomas's son, documentary evidence implies that it was built by ap Thomas, and there are features in the masonry detail that link the great tower to ap Thomas's other main building, the south gate. The tower originally had five storeys, but the upper level was destroyed following the castle's surrender after the civil war siege in the summer of 1646.

William Herbert, who was later executed in 1469 after the battle of Edgecote, continued the work of his father, but the bulk of the building programme may date to the 1460s, for from 1461 Herbert was a staunch supporter of the new king, Edward IV, and established himself as that monarch's right-hand man in Wales. The pinnacle of his career was reached when he was made earl of Pembroke in 1468, following his capture of the last Lancastrian stronghold in Wales, Harlech Castle (p. 35). He became one of the first Welshman to enter the ranks of the English peerage. Apart from the Elizabethan and Jacobean additions, the rest of the castle is the work of Herbert, although he never managed to complete the work. Around the Fountain Court were ranged a series of private apartments, backed by latrine towers, each room generally having a fireplace and a window. Herbert also built (or rebuilt) the chapel, which lay alongside the hall, flooring it with Malvern tiles.

There is a clear break in the masonry on the exterior curtain wall near the Kitchen Tower, a contrast between the superb fifteenth-century pale sandstone ashlar and the red sandstone rubble walling of the Elizabethan period. In the early sixteenth century Raglan was to pass through the female line to the Somerset family who were earls of Worcester. Most of the later work is ascribed to the third earl, William Somerset, with some additions by his son. In order to improve the accommodation, buildings were heightened and rooms built above the buttery. Also, a long gallery, an essential feature of any respectable great Tudor mansion, was added in the Fountain Court. Niches decorated with shellwork and housing the busts of Roman emperors, ornaments much in vogue at this time, were added to the moat walk around the keep, and elaborate gardens were created to the west and south of the castle, for which much evidence still survives.

During the English civil war the castle served as a major royalist base, since Henry Somerset (d.1646), first marquess of Worcester, was a staunch Roman Catholic and royalist. The castle was strengthened by a series of earthworks with bastions (platforms for artillery), but fell after a siege of a few weeks to the New Model Army under the command of Sir Thomas Fairfax. Thereafter, it was slighted and abandoned.

Raglan as a late medieval castle has few, if any, parallels in this country. The great detached keep with its two bascule drawbridges, the prominent machicolations and high degree of carved stonework around the state apartments all suggest continental influence, although the actual carved masonry itself has west country affinities. That both William ap Thomas and his son campaigned in France may serve as a clue as to the source of inspiration for the building of Raglan.

The main entrance to the castle was originally over a drawbridge and through the Great Gate, with its twin half-hexagonal towers, and so into the Pitched Stone Court. The gatehouse has circular gunloops, and the entrance passage, originally vaulted, was protected with two sets of doors and portcullises, as well as guard chambers. The battlements have machicolations, as does the Closet Tower to the right of the gatehouse.

The Pitched Stone Court contained the service range, with the kitchens, brewhouse and other rooms, and on the opposite side to it is the hall range and the buttery with accommodation above it. Toothing

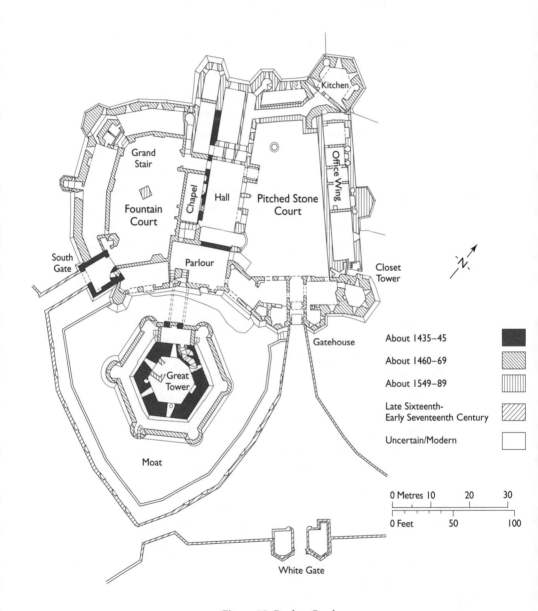

Figure 13: Raglan Castle

on the Kitchen and Closet towers indicates the alignment of the fifteenth-century office range, but the existing range dates to the following century, with its outer wall placed further out than its predecessor. Herbert's magnificent Kitchen Tower housed household staff on the upper floor, with the kitchen and servery on the ground floor, and a wet larder for raw meats in the basement, entered through its own doorway and down a steep flight of steps. Circular gunloops, similar to those in the gatehouse, can be seen in the Kitchen Tower, as well as in the Fountain Court.

Between the Kitchen Tower and the buttery is a short range and passage whose inner wall has long since disappeared. With accommodation above, it was once thought the ground floor housed the pantry, but it was more likely to have been for general storage. The passage continues into the buttery block, leading to one of three openings that ultimately led into the great hall. The central doorway, in the buttery itself, led to the serving hatch, while the third doorway, which is that nearest the Fountain Court, was used by those coming from the pantry, a room that lay under the Long Gallery.

Originally, on entering the hall range directly from either of the two courts, one would first have come to a passage screened off from the main body of the hall, hence the screens passage. The hall in its present form is Elizabethan, notably the fine recently restored oriel window at the dais end, overlooking the Pitched Stone Court. However, the building also retains much of its earlier walling. At the dais end, which was set below the plaque bearing the arms of the third earl of Worcester as a Knight of the Garter (after 1570), there was a doorway out to the private apartments, and this area also gave access to the wine and beer cellars.

The Fountain Court, so named from the fountain that once sat in the centre of the court, contains a range of apartments with fireplaces, handsome windows, as the one surviving indicates, and access to two latrine blocks. A grand staircase in the centre of the range provided the main access to the apartments. Backing on to the hall are the remains of the chapel, beyond which, on the other side of the remains of the hall porch, was the pantry. In the later sixteenth century a long gallery was built over the chapel and pantry, part of the once very fine fireplace still visible. A new staircase was built to give access to the gallery. This court could also be entered by William ap Thomas's south gate, which originally had a fine vaulted entrance passage.

The family's own private accommodation lay behind the hall range, with a parlour and a private dining room above it, immediately behind the hall, and bedchambers either side, all overlooking the great tower and its moat. The high status of this part of the castle is shown by the superbly carved masonry, including heraldic badges, around what remains of the windows.

Access to the great tower was gained over two bascule bridges, the smaller with a single arm, the larger with two. The arms were lifted into the vertical sockets in the tower's fabric. At some date the drawbridges were removed in favour of a fixed bridge that led into a forebuilding built against the keep. Stairs led down to the kitchen with its fireplace and well, as well as gunloops, and up to the private chambers above, all well appointed with fireplaces, fine windows and latrines. The great tower is surrounded by a turreted apron wall, one of the turrets having a latrine, another a doorway opening onto the moat. It is possible that, rather than being fifteenth-century work (as originally interpreted), the wall is part of the late sixteenth-/early seventeenth-century creation of the moat walk, a time that saw the development of the landscape that immediately surrounds the castle, with the creation of gardens, water gardens, terraces, lakes and walks. This was the period that saw the construction of the White Gate through which one enters the castle from the car park, and also the Red Gate, the foundations of which lie under the car park itself.

Recent work on the castle by historians, especially on the gardens, has transformed our knowledge of this great monument, but it has also shown that we have much more to unravel about Raglan's building history.

St Quentin's Castle, Llanblethian, Glamorgan

Ordnance Survey: Landranger 170. *SS: 989 742.* Cadw.

Although a castle has been here from the early twelfth century, built by the St Quentin family, the castle we see today dates to the early fourteenth century. However, behind the main surviving feature, the gatehouse, a mound of rubble marks the collapsed remains of a late Norman keep.

The castle came into the hands of the Clare family in the mid-thirteenth century, and it was the third Gilbert de Clare, who fell fighting the Scots at the battle of Bannockburn in 1314, who rebuilt the original castle. In the fifteenth and sixteenth centuries, the gatehouse was being used as a prison, thereafter falling into ruin. The central passage and ground-floor chambers were converted into a cottage in the nineteenth century before the castle once again became a ruin.

Gilbert III's castle was rectangular, with the main emphasis on display being placed on the east front, with the central twin-towered gatehouse projecting from the curtain wall, a polygonal south-east tower and a substantial rectangular one at the north-east corner, now both very ruinous indeed. Short stretches of curtain wall linked the towers to the gatehouse; that to the south is built to first-floor level, whilst the curtain to the north rises a level above.

The twin towers of the rectangular gatehouse have their sides chamfered; they may run down to meet spur buttresses typical of the period, but which now lie buried. The central passage had two gates, each with a portcullis, and a doorway on each side leading into guard chambers, each with four arrowslits. The chamber on the right or north side was smaller than its counterpart as behind it there is another doorway opening on to the staircase to the upper levels of the gate. The alterations to the arrowslits in the now inaccessible south chamber suggest that this was the prison from the later Middle Ages, while the fireplace built into what was a latrine chute dates to the cottage period.

The first floor may have been one room, served by a small fireplace and minimal lighting, unless timber partitions divided it. The south-west corner was a latrine chamber. Of the second floor, very little remains, but this may have provided the main accommodation, along with the north-east tower to which this level was linked.

Skenfrith Castle, Monmouthshire
See **The Three Castles**

Swansea Castle, Glamorgan

Ordnance Survey: Landranger 159. *SS: 657 931.*
Guidebook (Gower). Cadw.

All that remains of this once important castle, the centre of the lordship of Gower and built to command the original course of the river Tawe, is the late thirteenth-century Braose hall range, known as the 'New Castle', with the decorative arcading added in the first half of the fourteenth century, presumably by the Mowbrays. Similar arcading is still to be seen at two palaces in Pembrokeshire belonging to the bishop of St Davids, Lamphey and St Davids itself, but there is no evidence that Bishop Henry de Gower of St Davids (1328–47) was responsible for the work at Swansea.

The Norman castle lay to the north, probably originally a motte, although some have argued for a ringwork. This castle also had substantial masonry defences added during the thirteenth century. All this has long since gone, leaving us with the 'New Castle' that sits in the south-east corner of the outer ward. Both sides of the ruins can be inspected, but at present there is no access into the buildings themselves. A well is situated close to the medieval buildings.

A short stretch of curtain wall connects the two parts of the castle, the larger being the range with a first-floor hall. The other building is the much altered north-east tower, a building that was a debtors' prison from the eighteenth century until 1853, and architectural features from this later phase still survive. At the west end of the hall range is the tall latrine tower, against which is a stub of mid-thirteenth-century masonry. The main entrance to the first-floor hall was originally from an external stair, to the left of which is a late medieval stair turret built to link the hall with two of the three vaulted cellars beneath. The end of the range nearest the latrine turret was a service room with its own entrance, as well as three doorways into the hall. At the other end of the hall two doorways led into the lesser hall or solar, with a latrine at the end of a mural passage, but no fireplace, although there is one in one of two chambers below it.

The outstanding feature of the castle is on the outside, the arcaded parapet with arches in white Sutton stone, quarried from near Ogmore on the Vale of Glamorgan coast. Below the arcading are the windows of the hall range, with tall cross-slits below them, lighting the vaulted cellars.

The Three Castles – Grosmont, Skenfrith and White

Introduction

As the history of these three castles (figure 14) is inextricably linked into the twentieth century, it is logical to treat them together in one section.

Although the first documentary evidence relating to the Three Castles of White, Skenfrith and Grosmont is dated 1162–3, when over £19 was expended by the Crown, it is inconceivable that they did not exist by the early twelfth century. The territories of the Three Castles became as one early in King Stephen's reign (1135–54), following the Welsh uprising on the death of King Henry I in 1135. Thereafter, until the twentieth century, the Three Castles remained in single ownership, such was the strategic importance of these castles on the Anglo-Welsh border in the Middle Ages.

From 1177 to 1188 work is recorded at these sites. Some of the costs imply refurbishment of timber defences, such as the sum of about £15 at Grosmont in 1183–6, but at White (or Llantilio) Castle £128 16s. was spent in 1184–6, shortly after the partial destruction by the Welsh of Abergavenny Castle in 1182. This expenditure on White is likely to have been on the curtain wall of the inner ward, and possibly the keep, although that may have already been in existence. Over £43 was spent on works at Skenfrith in 1186, with repairs to the palisades undertaken in 1187.

In 1201 the lordship of the Three Castles entered a new era when they were granted by King John (1199–1216) to Hubert de Burgh (c.1175–1243), a distinguished soldier, and one who would have been well aware of castle developments across the Channel, as well as down the road at William Marshal's Chepstow. Apart from during Hubert's capture and imprisonment in France (1205–7), and the transfer of the lordship to William de Braose for a short period, he was free to develop Grosmont and Skenfrith, and the earliest masonry at these two castles dates to his time. The Norman development of White meant that Hubert considered additional work unnecessary. Hubert's work is assigned to two phases: 1201–4/5 (the 'hall' at Grosmont) and 1219–32 (all of Skenfrith and the curtain and mural towers at Grosmont); for work at Grosmont the king gave Hubert fifty oaks in 1227. The later phases at all three castles are considered in the descriptions below, works undertaken by the Crown in the mid-thirteenth century at White, and by the house of Lancaster in the fourteenth century at Grosmont.

Grosmont

Ordnance Survey: Landranger 161. *SO: 405 244.*
Guidebook. Cadw.

Although not very evident, the castle (figure 14) is approached through an outer ward. The gatehouse is of two builds; originally constructed by Hubert de Burgh after 1219 as a rectangular tower with rounded external corners, it was extended in the fourteenth century to provide a buttressed drawbridge pit, one of a number of improvements made by the Lancasters.

The rectangular range on the east side of the castle is usually interpreted as a first-floor hall and solar, with storage, kitchens et cetera on the ground floor. The hall was entered from an external timber stair, but staff in the service rooms could access the upper room from a spiral stair in the south-east corner. Both the hall and solar had fireplaces, and both rooms were well lit.

In the Hubert de Burgh second phase (after 1219), three mural towers were constructed, similar to those at Skenfrith, with deep basements, and arrowslits on the upper floors. However, in the fourteenth century two of the towers were altered and heightened, whilst the third, to the north, was demolished. A fine arch marks the fourteenth-century entrance to the south-west tower, with a spiral stair providing access to the upper floors (an external timber stair also led to the uppermost chambers). The rooms here both had fireplaces.

The north block, with its very fine octagonal chimney serving two fireplaces, was extended out from the curtain, the earlier mural tower being demolished to ground level and its basement infilled; a postern was also demolished at the same time. On either side of the mural tower the earls of Lancasters built a three-storey rectangular tower. Thus, the north block provided a high-status suite of rooms for the house of Lancaster. It was possibly Henry of Lancaster who built this range before 1330, or his son Henry of Grosmont, first duke of Lancaster, between 1334 and 1361. With the fine deer park associated with the castle, we can perhaps see Grosmont as a superior hunting lodge.

Skenfrith Castle

Ordnance Survey: Landranger 161. *SO: 457 202.*
Guidebook. Cadw.

The Norman castle, of which traces have been found in excavations and geophysical survey, was rebuilt in stone by Hubert de Burgh, probably some time after 1219 (apart from the tower in the centre of the west curtain, which dates to the later thirteenth century), perhaps at the time that the inner ward at Grosmont was being strengthened. Like White, the castle was encircled originally by a stone-revetted moat, but utilizing the river Monnow on the east (figure 14).

Skenfrith in plan is rectangular, with towers at each corner (the south-west tower now has an incorrect batter, dating to 1911–14), a gatehouse (all but vanished by the mid-eighteenth century) and a round keep in the middle of the ward, built on raised ground. A postern or water gate lies in the middle of the east curtain, and the kitchens, of uncertain date, lay to the south of it. On the west side of the ward lies the hall range, with the site of the chapel located between this range and the gatehouse.

In spite of Hubert de Burgh's knowledge of Chepstow and Dover, both Skenfrith and Grosmont lack twin-towered gatehouses. The curtain wall has a batter, unlike the mural towers, and has sockets for hourding at battlement level. The wall-walk is carried up via steps around the tops of the south towers. The mural towers had deep basements (a feature seen also at Grosmont) with two upper floors, presumably reached by a wooden staircase. These floors were provided with arrowslits, but no allowance was made for accommodation. One of the best surviving arrowslits, still with its ashlar, is to be seen in the north-east tower. Flanking the south-east tower is evidence for a possible latrine (to the left) and a postern (to the right).

The hall range was uncovered in the excavations during the 1950s. Until the lower level was filled in during the later Middle Ages, probably because of the problems of flooding, this building was of two storeys, with the hall and chamber on the top floor (the northern rooms are displayed at the original level). The gravel infilling led to the preservation of the original ironwork in one of the windows in this range.

The round keep dominates the interior, one of a number of such structures in the southern March of Wales, both English- and Welsh-built. There are traces of the original white plaster rendering on the exterior. A timber stair led to the first-floor entrance, with a mural stair leading to the upper floor and the battlements (the ground-floor opening is not regarded as an original feature). The main chamber was on the top floor, for it was provided with windows, a fireplace and a latrine.

Traces of a medieval wharf to the north of the castle were uncovered during work on consolidating the river bank in 2003. It possibly dates to the time of Hubert de Burgh.

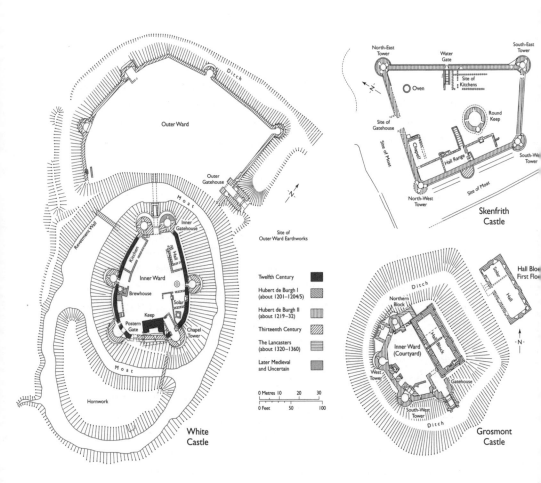

Figure 14: The Three Castles – Grosmont, Skenfrith and White

White

Ordnance Survey: Landranger 161. *SO: 379 167.*

Entry charge (April to October). Guidebook. Cadw.

The castle (figure 14) is entered as it would have been in the thirteenth century, through the outer ward with its solid-towered gatehouse (with drawbridge and portcullis) and on to the inner gatehouse. The original entrance in the twelfth century was from the south, across an earthwork (the 'hornwork') and through an entrance in the lee of a small square keep, of which only the footings remain.

The large outer ward has three rounded two-storey towers and also one rectangular one with accommodation at first-floor level indicated by a fireplace and latrine. Geophysical survey of the outer ward has revealed evidence for a large aisled barn, which suggests that the castle's key role in the twelfth and thirteenth centuries was as a military depot; metalworking in the Forest of Dean provided large quantities of crossbow bolts and other munitions. The masonry of the outer ward dates to the mid-thirteenth century, as do the gatehouse, revetment and mural towers of the inner ward.

The inner ward has a moat, the water levels being controlled by two dams to the south-east and north-west. Much of the face of the east tower of the inner gate is a rebuild of uncertain date, although the re-flooring of the gatehouse in 1437–8 may indicate the completion of repairs after the front had collapsed into the moat. Two gates and a portcullis secured the gate passage. Both towers were of four storeys.

Ranged around the inner ward, against the curtain, are the foundations of a number of buildings of uncertain date. There is a service range on the west side, with a kitchen and brewhouse, and a small building of two phases on the opposite side, interpreted as successive halls. The south-east mural tower housed the chapel; its piscina can be seen to the right of the central arrowslit.

The keep was still standing in 1256–7, as its roof was repaired then, but it was eventually demolished to make way for a stretch of curtain wall. The unusual arrangement of staggered horizontal slits of the arrowloops in the mural towers of the inner ward is to be seen in few other castles, and modern-day archers have said that this arrangement does help to improve the field of view.

Trellech, castle motte, Monmouthshire

Ordnance Survey: Landranger 162. *SO: 500 054*. Public footpath.

A public footpath allows a view of this small Norman motte in the village of Trellech. In the Middle Ages this was a large flourishing town, the importance of which is attested by the fine largely fourteenth-century church.

Tretower Castle and Court, Breconshire

Ordnance Survey: Landranger 161. *SO: 186 212*.
Entry charge. Guidebook. Cadw.

At the time of writing, this monument was about to become the centrepiece of a major Cadw project. The result of this work should see an enhanced interpretation, even reinterpretation, of the site, especially the Court, including a new guidebook, and this should be taken into account when using the following text.

The Castle

The castle and later house form one of the jewels in Cadw's crown, nestling as they do between the hills framing the Usk valley, at the south-western edge of the Black Mountains. The castle was founded by a Norman called Picard at the close of the eleventh century, and he built a motte and bailey close to a small stream. It was a later Picard who, some time in the twelfth century, converted the castle into a more formidable stronghold than it had been with its timber defences. The motte was lowered and a polygonal shell keep built to replace the palisade; the bailey, now a farmyard, retained its timber defences.

In the early thirteenth century, a circular keep was built by the Picards within the earlier curtain, necessitating the destruction of the Norman hall and solar and the blocking of various openings in order to thicken and heighten the twelfth-century shell keep to form a more formidable curtain wall. At the same time the bailey was given a stone curtain with mural towers. The Picards continued to hold the castle until the early fourteenth century, when it passed through the female line to the Bloets of Raglan and their descendants (see p. 134). Although the castle was ordered to be garrisoned during the Glyndŵr revolt, its role as a home was on the wane, the emphasis passing to the Court, a complex of buildings that evolved through to the seventeenth century.

The shell keep of the castle was entered through a small gate tower, a pit within it indicating that there was some form of drawbridge originally. Adjacent to the gate is a doorway that led up to the upper floor of the gate tower and the wall-walk. Within this stone enclosure was a kitchen at ground level, with a hall and small chamber or solar on the upper floor, reached by a staircase in the south-west corner. The kitchen continued to function after the round keep had been added, and visible on the outside are the little triangular ventilation holes to improve the draught up the fireplace's chimney.

The round keep consisted of four floors, including a basement, and was entered at first-floor level. It has the usual sloping or battered base to be seen on other great circular towers in Wales, at the top of which is a roll-moulded stringcourse. To enter the first floor one had to pass through two doorways, between which a mural stair led up to the upper floors. In order to descend to the basement originally, one had to enter the window embrasure opposite the main entrance and go down another mural staircase. The first floor had a fireplace as well as a second window, and there was a similar arrangement on the floor above. However, an additional feature at this level was a doorway that led to a bridge across to the wall-walk (it can be clearly seen from outside that the doorway was not placed centrally beneath the bridge roof).

The uppermost floor appears to be a slightly later addition, and had only two windows. The evidence that suggests the fourth floor was an addition can be found in a narrow window lighting the stairs up to that level, where the top half has been built askew to the bottom half.

Other features to note regarding the great tower is that there may have been a timber gallery or hourd projecting from the battlements, and there is a series of sockets in the external wall of the tower, the only surviving evidence for a timber building of uncertain date added between the keep and the curtain wall.

The Court

Tretower Court was in the hands of the Vaughan family in the middle of the fifteenth century, and Sir Roger began to make extensive improvements to the building. The north range, which is fourteenth century in origin and presumably replaced the castle as a more comfortable place to dwell, originally contained a hall open to the roof. Sir Roger transformed it by flooring over the hall to make a complete first-floor suite of rooms: hall, solar and bedroom, as well as a guest apartment at the east end, the whole block being served with three latrines. A gallery or balcony was added on the courtyard side. A new, west, wing ran south from the kitchen of the north range. Sir Thomas Vaughan continued his father's work by enclosing the courtyard on the south and east, constructing a small gatetower.

In the early seventeenth century, the Vaughans made some modifications, including roofing the wall-walk on the south side; new windows were added, and the south end of the west range became the principal living area. Possibly about this time, a garden to the south and west was laid out, surrounded by a low wall.

The Court passed out of the hands of the Vaughan family in the later eighteenth century, becoming a farm, until it passed into state care in 1930, courtesy of the Brecknock Society.

The main entrance to the Court was through the central passage of the gatehouse, although a smaller doorway immediately to the north provided day-to-day pedestrian access, as it does today. A staircase off the gate passage led up to the first floor of the gate and the wall-walk. On entering the courtyard, there is the north range on the right, with storage rooms at ground level and a cellar which may have housed a cider press. The original kitchen lay at the west end of the range. Above was the private suite of rooms for the Vaughans in the fifteenth century, which were later generally used for private accommodation in the Tudor and early Stuart periods.

The west range, opposite the gatehouse, has a hall open to the very fine roof, with service rooms beyond and a kitchen, described as the mess hall. On the north side of the hall is a solar or private chamber, though it backs on to what has been interpreted as the original kitchen, but perhaps this is unlikely. This 'kitchen' and its upper chamber were both served by fireplaces and latrines.

On the other side of the hall were service rooms, screened off from the hall, used in the preparation of food and drink, and at the far end the so-called mess hall for retainers – or was this always a kitchen, from whence food entered the service rooms, and so passed on to the hall, rather than a hall connected to a kitchen only from the early seventeenth century?

In the early seventeenth century the first floor of the south end of the west range was upgraded to provide finer accommodation for the Vaughan family, with large windows and fireplaces.

Twmbarlwm, castle motte, Risca, Monmouthshire

Ordnance Survey: Landranger 171. *ST: 243 926.* Open access.

On a hill above Newport, and visible for miles around, is a large motte in what appears to have been an exposed and bleak position. The motte may have been little more than support for a watchtower, and it has been suggested that it may have even been built as late as the end of the thirteenth century. A bank and ditch delineate a bailey, although the vast area of this would suggest that the bailey may in origin have been an Iron Age hillfort.

Usk Castle, Monmouthshire

Ordnance Survey: Landranger 171. *SO: 377 011.*
Entry charge. Guidebook. Privately owned.

The late eleventh-century earth-and-timber castle was transformed into a masonry structure by William Marshal (d.1219). Marshal had acquired the Clare estates, including Chepstow, in 1189 through his marriage to Isabella de Clare, the daughter of Richard de Clare (d.1176), known as Strongbow. Before 1189, the castle had been in the hands of the Crown during Isabella's minority, although a local Welsh lord, Hywel ab Iorwerth, held it for a short period. King Henry II spent over £10 on repairs to the castle buildings in 1185.

In 1189, there was one major stone building in the castle, the 'keep' at the entrance to the inner ward (but see below). As with many small Norman keeps in south Wales, the building is in an 'offensive' position, on the line of the later curtain wall, which must follow the line of the timber palisade. Probably dating to the later twelfth century, it is usually considered that it was built by Strongbow. It was much altered at different periods of the Middle Ages (for example, the north wall was rebuilt in the fifteenth century), but it eventually consisted of two floors over a basement; two double-splayed Norman windows, now blocked, survive in the south wall.

However, it seems that the history of this building mirrors the main towers at such castles as Ludlow in Shropshire and Richmond in Yorkshire. In the east wall of Usk's tower there is evidence for an arch, which would imply that the 'keep' was originally a gate tower, later blocked to form a 'keep' or large mural tower when the present entrance was created by Marshal a few metres to the west. So, originally the gate tower had one room above the entrance passage. The second floor was added in the thirteenth century and a doorway created to link it with the new latrine turret at the south-west corner.

William Marshal transformed the castle in the early thirteenth century, although later additions and loss of fabric partially obscure the castle of this period. The curtain wall dates to this time, as does the round Garrison Tower on the south-west side of the inner ward and the equally large, but fragmentary, round tower to the south-west of it. The Garrison Tower is of four storeys and overlooks the town. The original entrance was at first-floor level, reached by a timber staircase. The lower two floors have arrowslits, whilst the upper two have lancet windows, and all levels are linked by a spiral stair; the wall-walk could be accessed from the third floor.

It has been suggested that the alterations to the Garrison Tower (including the ground-floor doorway, the upper storey and the battlements) were undertaken by Gilbert II de Clare, earl of Gloucester, the builder of Caerphilly (p. 100), at the time when he was building the D-shaped north tower, where the earl kept his 'treasure'. However, it has been suggested recently that these alterations date to the time of his son, Gilbert III (d.1314), in 1308–9. The other building from Gilbert III's time is probably what came to be called the 'Countess's Chamber', a rectangular block built out from the northern curtain.

A number of domestic buildings were built by Gilbert's widow, Countess Matilda, from 1315 until her death in 1320, including the hall and chapel against the northern curtain, possibly completing the work that her husband had started. On Matilda's death the lordship of Usk passed to her sister-in-law, Elizabeth de Burgh (d.1360), and she and her husband continued the work on the castle, including the provision of an oriel window for the goldsmith next to the Countess's Chamber. In the outer ward a new gatehouse was built, and over £10 was spent on the construction of two drawbridges, whilst ditches were cleaned out and watchtowers were repaired. This activity is likely to be related to the revolt in 1321 by the Marcher lords, including Roger Dammory,

Elizabeth's husband, against Hugh Despenser, the king's favourite. The revolt was initially successful, but by early 1322 the king and Despenser were back in control – Elizabeth was taken prisoner in January and her husband died two days after his capture in March.

It was not until 1326 that Elizabeth regained Usk from the Despensers. Repairs were then undertaken, for Elizabeth made several visits to Usk from this time to about 1350. The accounts that survive detail work on new chambers and latrines, a stable in the outer ward and a bell tower, as well as carpentry work, plastering and other activities. It was threatened, but not taken, during Owain Glyndŵr's revolt in 1405, and some later fifteenth-century work included the north wall of the Norman keep.

The castle was used as a residence until the middle of the sixteenth century, before it fell into disrepair. The outer ward, with its gardens and fine gatehouse, is part of the private accommodation of the owners and is not usually accessible.

Weobley Castle, Glamorgan

Ordnance Survey: Landranger 159. *SS: 478 928.*
Entry charge. Guidebook (Gower). Cadw.

This castle-cum-fortified manor house sits amongst the splendour of the north Gower coast, with views across to Carmarthenshire and Pembrokeshire, and below it lies the expanse of the Llanrhidian marsh. It was built in the early fourteenth century by the de la Bere family, although this work was undertaken in two phases. Improvements were made in the late fifteenth century by Sir Rhys ap Thomas, whose main residence was at Carew Castle (p. 62). In particular, he built the porch block, to make a grander entrance to the hall range, reminiscent of work that he undertook at Carew. Minor modifications were made to the area of the first floor between the hall and the east range in the late sixteenth century, and it was from this time through into the last century that Weobley was occupied as a farmhouse by tenants, although owned by the Mansel and then the Talbot families of Margam.

Approaching the castle, a modest gateway (doors, but no portcullis) sits between the cistern turret to the right and the solar range to the left; this west front dates to the second de la Bere phase.

The cistern turret, so called because rainwater may have been channelled to a cistern in the basement, was built against the south-west tower of the first phase.

On entering the small courtyard it can be seen that on the other side of the south-west tower are the remains of a rectangular building that may have had a chapel on the first floor, judging by the remains of a piscina found in excavations. This building, too, was erected against the south-west tower, which was initially freestanding. Beyond the chapel are the footings of the south-east tower, built over a kiln that provided lime for the preparation of mortar used in building Weobley. The tower was planned to have at least three floors judging by the latrine chutes, but it was probably never completed. Further latrines were provided in the polygonal turret at the north end of the east range, the latter providing family or guest accommodation on the first floor, with the ground floor put to household use. In the late fifteenth century a second floor was added by lowering the first floor.

It is the hall and solar ranges on the north and north-west sides that are the best-surviving parts of the castle. The hall later lay on the first floor, with a kitchen below, although initially it appears that both the hall and the kitchen were at ground level. Wrapped across the hall block and its link with the east range on the courtyard side is the porch range added at the end of the fifteenth century. At the west end of the hall a doorway opened into the solar, which had a cellar beneath it, and from the solar a passage provided access to a chamber above the gate, and on to a latrine. The solar itself was the private chamber of the de la Bere family, and had a fireplace and fine windows overlooking the courtyard and the marshes.

All together Weobley would have been a compact and comfortable strong house, although not strong enough to resist the Welsh in 1403 during the Glyndŵr revolt, but then many an actual castle fell to Welsh at this time also.

White Castle, Monmouthshire
See **The Three Castles**

7

Aftermath

The passing of the Middle Ages did not see the end of the construction of castle-like structures. In fact we have already seen with Cardiff and Castell Coch in Glamorgan (pp. 110, 111) the romantic idealization of the medieval world, with the work of William Burges on behalf of the marquess of Bute. This has not been the book to discuss the architecture of the post-medieval and early modern period, other than where it has directly impinged on a medieval castle, such as Raglan and Chirk, but it would be remiss not to mention some of the later buildings that are called castles.

We find this almost throwback to the Middle Ages elsewhere in Glamorgan, for on the hills above Cardiff stands Ruperra Castle, a rectangular building with tower at each corner (one has collapsed). Built in the 1620s, it is now inaccessible and in danger of collapse, although Ruperra's Friends are valiantly fighting its cause. John Newman, in his work on Glamorgan's buildings (1995), describes it as follows: 'This splendidly direct and uncompromising building is an outstanding example of the nostalgia for the chivalric past felt in the early C17.'

It is in north Wales, however, that we find the best examples of the nineteenth-century castle revival. Although just across the border in Cheshire, the classic site, and arguably the finest of them, is Peckforton Castle, on a hill opposite medieval Beeston Castle, designed by the great architect Anthony Salvin and built in 1844–50. Peckforton is a late example of a sham castle, for two in Wales had already been built: Gwrych in Denbighshire and Bodelwyddan in Flintshire. Gwrych was begun in 1819 and largely finished in 1822, but there were later alterations and, as with so many of these great nineteenth-century piles, it has undergone various vicissitudes in its existence. It has numerous towers, as well as gatehouses and a barbican and there are also a number of castellated lodges and estate buildings round about, built slightly later than the main house.

Bodelwyddan was 'castellated' in the 1830s, again with towers and gatehouse, but a slightly earlier example of this medieval revivalism in south Wales is Cyfarthfa Castle on the edge of Merthyr Tydfil, built for the great industrialist William Crawshay in 1824–5.

These castles are all in the tradition of the thirteenth-century castle, but we find the Romanesque or twelfth-century Norman style at another 'castle' in north Wales, Penrhyn near Bangor in Caernarfonshire, built 1827–40. Although there are a variety of differently shaped towers, it is the grand 'Norman' keep that dominates the castle, its inspirations being the fine Norman tower of Castle Hedingham in Essex.

One man who wanted to rebuild an existing medieval castle in Wales was Sir Samuel Rush Meyrick, primarily for his son, but also to exhibit his extraordinary collection of arms and armour. Carew and Llansteffan castles were considered, but in the event this did not prove possible. Instead, he built Goodrich Court on the Welsh border in Herefordshire in 1828–31, opposite one of the finest medieval castles of the Marches. The latter survives, but Goodrich Court was demolished in the middle of the twentieth century, although the lodge still stands by the Ross to Monmouth road.

Although these nineteenth-century buildings do hark back to the Middle Ages, there is something cold and clinical about the pastiche that does not appeal to this writer. It is far better to glory in what was created in the Middle Ages. A modern and confident Wales can justly be proud of this medieval heritage, even if the country's most Welsh town has to suffer having Edward I's brooding citadel dominating its streets; however, one just has to recall the events of 1294!

Regnal and other Dates

Dafydd ap Gruffudd, prince, d.1283
Edward the Confessor, king of England, 1042–66
Edward I, king of England, 1272–1307
Edward II, king of England, 1307–27
Edward III, king of England, 1327–77
Gilbert II de Clare, earl of Gloucester, d.1295
Gilbert III de Clare, earl of Gloucester, d.1314
Gruffudd ap Cynan, king of Gwynedd, d.1137
Henry I, king of England, 1100–35
Henry II, king of England, 1154–89
Henry III, king of England, 1216–72
Henry V, king of England, 1413–22
Henry VII, king of England, 1485–1509
Hubert de Burgh, justiciar of England, d.1243
John, king of England, 1199–1216
Llywelyn ab Iorwerth (Fawr, the Great), c.1173 –1240
Llywelyn ap Gruffudd, prince of Wales, d.1282
Owain Glyndŵr, prince, d.c.1415/16
Owain Gwynedd, king of Gwynedd, d.1170
Rhys ap Gruffudd, the Lord Rhys, prince of Deheubarth, d.1197
Rhys ap Tewdwr, king of Deheubarth, d.1093
Richard fitz Gilbert de Clare (Strongbow), earl of Pembroke, d.1176
Robert fitz Hamon, lord of Glamorgan, d.1107
Roger Bigod, fifth earl of Norfolk, d.1306
Stephen, king of England, 1135–54
William I, king of England, 1066–87
William II, king of England, 1087–1100
William Marshal, earl of Pembroke, d.1219

Further Reading

There is a vast amount of recent literature on castles, and for details see the writer's *Castles, Town Defences and Artillery Fortifications in the United Kingdom: A Bibliography 1945–2006* (Donington, 2008). General material, including publications specifically on Wales as a whole, can be found in Part 1 (pp. 5–86), with castles in the Welsh counties on pp. 348–435. An appendix covers material published while the book was in production (pp. 659–73). The castles themselves are listed by historic county, but for those unfamiliar with these, there is an index of sites.

For a general history of Wales, see the book by J. G. Jones in the Pocket Guide series by the University of Wales Press, *The History of Wales*, 2nd edition (Cardiff, 1998).

For a general introduction to castle architecture, R. A. Brown's *English Castles* (London, 1976; reprinted as *Allen Brown's English Castles* in 2004) is still of use. A short book by O. Creighton and R. Higham is also an invaluable introduction: *Medieval Castles* (Princes Risborough, 2003), one of the Shire Archaeology series. For town defences see the same authors' *Medieval Town Walls* (Stroud, 2005). The archaeology of castles is treated in my *Medieval Fortifications* (Leicester, 1990; reprinted, London, 2005).

A number of the Welsh counties have had detailed studies made of their castles. There is nothing to rival the two-volume survey of Glamorgan castles by the Royal Commission on the Ancient and Historical Monuments of Wales, published in 1991 (*Early Castles*) and 2000 (*Later Castles*). The Herefordshire publisher, Logaston Press, has a county series titled Monuments in the Landscape, and four of the volumes cover the castles of Breconshire, Glamorgan, Pembrokeshire and Radnorshire.

A number of official county histories include coverage of castles and, in particular, the reader should note the medieval volumes for the counties of Glamorgan, Merioneth, Monmouthshire and Pembrokeshire. Other counties are covered by papers published in the annual journals of county historical and archaeological societies, such as those for Breconshire, Cardiganshire and Montgomeryshire.

The Pevsner Architectural Guides, covering an individual county's or group of counties' buildings, originally published by Penguin, but now by Yale University Press, began to describe Wales in 1979 with *Powys* (Breconshire, Montgomeryshire and Radnorshire). *Clwyd* (Denbighshire and Flintshire) appeared in 1986, followed by *Glamorgan* (1995), *Gwent/Monmouthshire* (2000), *Pembrokeshire* (2004) and *Carmarthenshire* and *Ceredigion* (2006). The final volume, *Gwynedd* (Anglesey, Caernarvonshire and Merioneth), appeared in 2009.

The Cadw series, 'A guide to ancient and historic Wales', appeared in four volumes from 1992 to 1995, and full coverage of the major castles is included.

For an understanding of the actual building of the castles of King Edward I in mid and north Wales, see Arnold Taylor's *The Welsh Castles of Edward I* (London, 1986) originally published as part of R. A. Brown, H. M. Colvin and A. J. Taylor, *The History of the King's Works. 1–2. The Middle Ages* (London, 1963). The following should also be consulted: D. M. Williams and J. R. Kenyon (eds), *The Impact of the Edwardian Castles in Wales* (Oxford, 2010).

Richard Avent's *Cestyll Tywysogion Gwynedd/Castles of the Princes of Gwynedd* remains one of the best introductions to the castles of the Welsh princes (Cardiff, 1983), but see also Paul Davis's *Castles of the Welsh Princes* (Talybont, 2007).

For individual castles, the best source is the guidebook, and few, if any, can be bettered than those published by Cadw on the castles in state care in Wales.

In order to understand the work that was involved in the construction of our abbeys and castles, see Nicola Coldstream's *Builders & Decorators: Medieval Craftsmen in Wales*, published by Cadw (Cardiff, 2008).

As has been intimated in this book, there is so much more to castles than the fortifications and, to understand the service operations that went on in the great households, one can do no better than to read Peter Brears's *Cooking and Dining in Medieval England* (Totnes, 2008).

Finally, I must wholeheartedly recommend to any researcher the online resources of the Royal Commission on the Ancient and Historical Monuments of Wales, with the National Monuments Record Wales (NMRW), (*www.rcahmw.gov.uk*). Coflein (*www.coflein.gov.uk*) is the online database for the NMRW, the national collection of information about the historic environment of Wales, and allows access to details of many thousands of archaeological sites, monuments, buildings and maritime sites in Wales, together with an index to the drawings, manuscripts and photographs held in the NMRW archive collections.

Index